DICK REED

HOW
TO LIVE
THE
VICTORIOUS
LIFE

HOW TO LIVE THE VICTORIOUS LIFE

By an Unknown Christian

Author of
THE KNEELING CHRISTIAN

ZONDERVAN PUBLISHING HOUSE
OF THE ZONDERVAN CORPORATION
GRAND RAPIDS, MICHIGAN 49506

First paperback printing   1966
Twentieth printing   1980
ISBN 0-310-33482-9

Printed in the United States of America

CONTENTS

Preface

AUTHOR'S PREFACE

Most men hesitate to speak of their own spiritual experiences. They are deterred by the fear of making "self" too prominent, or are ashamed to confess how much practical unbelief and half-hearted allegiance to their Lord exist in their lives.

The writer of this book knows his own unworthiness; but he humbly believes that he also knows something of the worthiness of an All-sufficient Saviour.

The manner in which this knowledge came — through an apparently trivial incident — is itself remarkable.

The immediate result was a joy which no bridling could restrain. But whenever this Victorious Life was spoken of, requests were made for "something in print." After much pressure from many directions, and with much hesitation on the part of the writer, he ventured to put down his reflections.

These appeared in the columns of *The Life of Faith,* through the kindness of the Editor.

They are here republished with practically no alterations. These chapters show the pathway by which one seeking soul found its way from "life" to "life more abundant."

They endeavour to reveal the helps and the hindrances which a seeker after the Victorious Life should know.

The writer owes much to the lives of four men, but the great "CRISIS" in his spiritual life took place, not in the uplift of a great convention, but in the quietude of his own study.

He believes that his experience is that of tens of thousands of Christian men and women — who have LIFE, and are earnest and devoted workers, yet who long for some Power which will conquer the so-called "little sins."

That POWER is the Lord Jesus Christ — and HE offers Himself to us (John 1:12).

So this book goes forth with much earnest prayer that others may be helped by the things which have been such an unspeakable inspiration to the writer, who — lest any shadow of self should fall upon these pages — humbly craves to be allowed to remain

AN UNKNOWN CHRISTIAN

Chapter I

IS IT POSSIBLE?

Is there such a Life? St. John plainly says that every child of God "overcometh the world."

Now *that* is Victory! And he tells us how Victory is secured: "This is the VICTORY that overcometh the world — even our faith" (1 John 5:4) — and then most of us give up in despair!

It all seems too vague — too indefinite. Besides, isn't our faith too small or too weak? Or perhaps we don't possess the "right kind of faith" to get the Victory.

With many of us there is a sneaking idea that the schoolboy was very near the mark when he said, "Faith is believing what ain't." But of this we are sure: to most Christians the Victorious Life is a beautiful mirage which vanishes into thin air, or recedes into the distance as we try to approach it. And so we look forward to finding it in heaven!

Now St. John isn't speaking about Victory in heaven — for *there,* "faith is *lost* in sight."

So there must be a Victory here on earth, in some way the result of faith. The writer would gladly give all he had in the world if in exchange he could have seen this way of Victory 25 years ago! After many years of Bible study, after many years of futile "struggling with temptation" which, with monotonous regularity, tested him, he at last saw a way out — or rather a way IN. It was to him a new way — a LIVING way — and eagerly he entered in. He now sees there is such a thing as Victory, and he marvels how he missed his way before. In the joy of — to him — a wonderful discovery he longs for others to share the blessing — in these "last days." And is there not a real heartfelt yearning amongst Christians today to lay hold — not on *life*, for they have that — but on *"life more abundant"*?

The Victorious Life! The words ring with hope. Moreover, wherever an announcement is made that such a topic is to be talked about, men and women flock to discover the secret of such a life. For they *know* intuitively that when *Victory* comes defeat goes! Those sad fluctuations — "up and down" experiences — in the spiritual life which are so depressing will go. Those shameful betrayals of the Master, which are so discouraging, will vanish away.

With Victory will come PEACE — a peace which really passeth all understanding.

With Victory will come JOY — a rejoicing with joy unspeakable and full of glory (1 Peter 1:8).

With Victory will come POWER — the very "power of God." The Victorious Life — a life of Peace, and Joy, and Power. Would not *such* a life satisfy any man?

Can we ask for anything better? And Christ offers *this*.

The writer proposes to try to make it plain and clear to the simplest mind, what the Bible says about this Life. We shall ask: How can it be obtained and retained? What are its difficulties and its dangers? Can it be lost? If so, can it be regained? We shall speak of real Victory and *false*. We hope to tell of its Triumphs and its Testings. Now we wish

To Give a Warning

It is this: Satan will do his utmost to cloud your mind. He will bring all sorts of doubts and difficulties to light. Why is this? Just because he is eager to prevent you from gaining Victory! Believe me, the devil does not mind your being "religious," and he does not mind how much *powerless* work you attempt so long as you fall short of the Victorious Life.

So long as you go to the world for your pleasures, and so long as you fall into the usual sins of respectable people, *the more you attempt for Christ* the more the *devil is pleased*. He simply revels in seeing defeated, worldly Christians desperately busy for Christ. But the devil will do his level best to discredit Victorious Life teaching and to keep you from even *seeking* to understand it. He is quite an adept in using — *i.e.*, misusing — Scripture.

But be confident of this very thing — that the teaching is striking home and striking him — the devil — when difficulties are suggested to your mind or some verse of Scripture "comes" to you, which seems to contradict some statement made in these chapters.

No one is more anxious than the writer that only the truth as it is in Christ Jesus shall be heard. If any statement is not true to Scripture or to experience, none will be more delighted to have this pointed out than the writer, who is possessed with a consuming desire that every Christian shall be "filled with all the fulness of God."

Chapter II

CAN "LITTLE" SINS BE CONQUERED?

The Victorious Life is a Life of Victory over Sin. Is such a thing possible? It is not a question of absolute sinlessness like that of Christ, or that of Adam before the fall. There will always remain the clear declaration of St. John: "If we say that we have no sin, we deceive ourselves."

Is Victory Promised Us?

The question we are facing is this — Can we obtain Victory over known, voluntary sin? Is any such hope of victory taught in the Bible? Is it ever experienced — lived out — by men today? If so, can *any* believer in Jesus Christ have Victory over all known sin — say, for one whole day — or is such Victory only for our spiritual leaders?

Surely these questions are often in men's minds. We *want* such Victory and even the Church of England teaches us to pray daily, "Vouchsafe, O Lord, to keep us this day, *without sin*." "Grant that this day we fall into *no sin*." Our Lord Himself taught us to pray, "Deliver us from evil" — or the evil one — *i.e.*, sin, or the author of sin. In the Church Catechism we teach our children that in this prayer we are asking God to "keep us from all sin and wickedness." Does

Christ or any branch of His Church bid us ask for an impossibility? If these prayers are not a mockery then a Victorious Life is possible.

But come down to everyday life. Can we think of any *one sin* over which Victory has never been won? We have seen drunkards turning to Christ, and *in a moment* getting absolute Victory over strong drink. Such men often declare not only that they have never fallen again, but that *the very desire* for alcohol has been entirely taken away. This is miraculous. So with other great besetting sins — God has given instantaneous and complete Victory.

If then we can get Victory over some deep-rooted, besetting sin, cannot our Saviour make us Victorious over the sins we sometimes regard as "little"? Christian people, as a rule, *i.e.*, in the great majority of cases, are *not* drunken, or vicious, or immoral.

But this can also be said of very many worldly and irreligious people. Isn't it true that there is little to choose between the average Christian and the ordinary moral "worldly" man? So the latter says, "What will it profit me to become a Christian?" And what can we say in reply? What would the worldly man gain? And what would others benefit by the change in him?

Under the Tyranny of Sin

Do we see any signs of the Victorious Life in the majority of professing Christians? In any flourishing Church, how many of its members exhibit a glowing love of souls and a burning zeal for Christ? We merely ask the question.

In how many do we see Victory over so-called *respectable* sins — bad temper, irritability, pride, jealousy, backbiting, unlove, *anxiety?*

Now we ask in all humility, Is there any remedy? Is there any hope of getting the Victorious Life? That is, a life of habitual Victory over sins ("small" as well as great) — a life of constant and conscious fellowship with God?

If such a hope can be found, it will be in God's Holy Word. Is it there?

"Victory over known sin! Can I get it?" What a momentous question! If we can get it for an hour — or a day — then why not *habitually?* Dare we ask every reader to put aside all ideas of his own on such a question? Will you approach it with an unprejudiced and unbiased mind? For the time being just shelve any preconceived ideas you may have on this subject. Forget all your own failures — and the faults of other Christians. Yes — and forget all *theories* of holiness. Simply allow God's written Word to speak for itself. Surely this is not an unfair demand?

A Promise and a Command

What does the New Testament talk about chiefly? By far the greatest part of it is devoted to telling Christians how to live after they have found Christ as their Saviour, rather than how to *get salvation* from the penalty of sin.

Before our Lord was born, the Angel of the Lord said of Him, "Thou shalt call His name Jesus for He shall save His people *from their sins*" (Matt. 1:21).

Quite early in His ministry Christ Himself said to His disciples, "Be ye therefore perfect even as your Father which is in heaven is perfect" (Matt. 5:48).

This must mean *something*. The Saviour would never command an impossibility. Here He definitely bids us possess some sort of "perfection" — in fact a perfection in *some way* like that of God the Father.

It is very wonderful and at first sight it seems impossible — incomprehensible. But *there is the command*.

Peter, speaking by the Holy Spirit, gives a very similar exhortation: "But LIKE as He which called you is holy, be ye yourselves also holy in all manner of living; because it is written 'Ye shall be holy, for I am holy' " (1 Peter 1:15).

We are then definitely commanded to possess some sort of "holiness" — in fact a holiness like that of Jesus Christ.

The writer of the Epistle to the Hebrews shows how important this is. "Follow peace," says he, "with all men, and holiness, *without which no man can see the Lord*" (Heb. 12:14).

15

John tells us plainly that he is writing his first Epistle so that its readers "may not sin" (1 John 2:1).

May we very humbly ask whether it is presumption on our part to inquire into the meaning of these words?

Where Presumption Lies

It surely *would be presumption* to doubt the possibility of our carrying out any command of Jesus Christ or the Holy Spirit? Ought not every sincere follower of the Lord Jesus to try to discover what these verses of Scripture mean?

Are you looking for the Return of Jesus Christ? Is that your hope? Well, more than 1,900 years ago John said, "Everyone that hath this hope set on Him, purifieth himself, EVEN AS HE IS PURE" (1 John 3:3).

St. John expects to find in Christians a purity somehow like Christ's!

"Whosoever is begotten of God doeth no sin . . . he cannot sin . . . " (1 John 3:9).

We have not referred to Paul's declarations on the same subject. "Reckon ye yourselves to be dead unto sin . . . sin shall *not* have dominion over you" (Rom. 6:11 and 14).

He tells us how it is done. "The shield of faith wherewith ye shall be able to quench ALL the fiery darts of the Evil one" (Eph. 6:16).

Do not our hearts burn within us at the very *thought* of such a life as is held out here?

Now whatever we may think about these words from Scripture — whatever our prejudices, whatever our past failures — however impossible it all seems — we cannot deny the following facts. In the Bible: God's Word:

1. There is a perfection commanded, in some way like that of God the Father.

2. There is a holiness enjoined like that of God Himself.

3. There is a purity offered, like that of Jesus Christ.

4. There is a *possibility* shown of resisting every attack of the evil one.

The life which such "perfection," such holiness, such

purity, and such power would produce would surely be a Victorious Life. Are we willing to study the question further? We are absolutely certain that God would not mock us by commanding an impossible standard, or by offering us something He is not able to give.

The question is NOT "Can *I* live a Victorious Life?" (We all know what the answer to that question is.) No! The thing which concerns me, is just this: "Can Jesus Christ *make* me holy — *keep* me holy — *give* me Victory?" If He can — shall we not get it? And then, shall we not cry out with St. Paul — in all exultation and yet withal, in all humility and adoration —

Thanks be unto God which giveth us the VICTORY through our Lord Jesus Christ (1 Cor. 15:57).

CHAPTER III

GOD'S LOVE NEVER FAILETH

What is the Victorious Life? It is the life of holiness, or the "perfect" life which is so often referred to by Paul in his Epistles.

Surely then the very first thing for us to do is to find out just what is commanded us, and promised us, in the New Testament. Two very definite things have been already spoken of — HOLINESS and PERFECTION. What do these words mean? And is "Holiness" the same thing as "Perfection"?

Now it is a very singular fact that really devoted — yet *defeated* — Christians gladly aim at "holiness," but are frightened of "perfection." "There is no such thing as 'perfection' " is a common remark on the lips of Christian people. Our reply is, that our Lord *commanded* it, whatever it is.

"Perfection" Here and Now

"Perfection," said a Professor of Theology, "is an unrealizable ideal towards which we progress through all eternity." Yet Christ demands some sort of "perfection" *here* and *now*. If we are really sincere we shall try to see what the Saviour means. "Be ye therefore 'perfect,' " said Christ.

"That's a bewildering command," was the comment

made on this verse, by a modern preacher, "but when our Lord adds, 'as your heavenly Father is perfect' we are simply staggered, and in despair give up attempting to obey!" Yet these added words are the key to the solution of the difficulty! For at once we can cut out all false ideas of "perfection."

How is our Heavenly Father "perfect"? Surely in everything. But He is *God* and we are *men*. He does not command us to be "perfect" as God. The FATHER is "perfect" in absolute sinlessness; in Majesty, in Glory, in Power, in Wisdom. Such "perfection" cannot be attained by mortal man. In what then are *we* to be "perfect"? "Be ye *therefore* perfect." That word "therefore" evidently refers to what has been said just before. What is that? Simply a command to be full of love. Godless men love their friends: the followers of Christ are to *love their enemies* as well. Our Lord is commanding perfect LOVE. This thought came to me with overwhelming power. The Victorious Life is simply a life of *perfect love*.

Our Lord's "New Commandment"

Towards the end of His earthly life our Lord said, "A new commandment I GIVE unto you, that ye *love* one another; even AS *I* HAVE LOVED YOU, that ye also love one another. By this shall all men know that ye are My disciples, if ye have love one to another" (John 13:34). There is the standard and there is the command to reach it.

As Christ loved — that is the standard; and that is perfect love. And this is commanded *us*. And St. Paul reminds us that "love" is the only thing which can enable us to obey God. "Love is the fulfilling of the Law" (Rom. 13:10).

"The point is, can an imperfect man or woman have 'perfect' love?" That was the opening sentence of an address on this subject. But surely that is not the way to approach this question? It is the blessed Master Who commands. It is not for me to cast even the shadow of a doubt on the possibility of what He bids. But, do we not feel constrained to cry out, like

20

a seeker of old, "How CAN these things be?" Is there such a thing as "perfect love"?

Assuredly there is. The Father's love is "perfect." The love wherewith Christ loved us is perfect. Human love is imperfect and always will be. But does not the Bible say, "The love of God hath been shed abroad in our hearts" (Rom. 5:5)? Would you believe it, if you were told that this was the reason why Jesus Christ revealed God the Father? Yet it is so. We have His own words for it.

Our Lord said, "I have made known unto them Thy name, and will make it known" — that includes you and me — "that the *love* wherewith Thou lovest Me, may be IN THEM, and I in them" (John 17:26).

The Secret — "Perfect Love"

Here, then, is the secret of it all. "Perfect love" is surely possible, but only possible when Jesus Christ Himself — God Himself Who is love — comes to dwell in our hearts.

St. John, the Apostle of love, told us this long ago. "If we LOVE one another God abideth IN US, and His love is perfected *in us*" (1 John 4:12).

"We *know* and have believed the love which God hath IN US. God is love; and he that abideth in love, abideth in God, and God abideth in him. Herein is love made PERFECT with us" (1 John 4:16,17). It is, therefore, as clear as day, that if we desire "perfect love," we *can get it* by having Jesus Christ — Who is love — filling our whole being. Then, and then only, can we understand that stupendous comparison of John: "because as He is, even so are WE in this world" (v. 17).

No wonder St. Paul cried out exultantly — defiantly? — "Who shall separate us from the love of God?" (Rom. 8:39). No wonder he bursts out in triumphant faith, when he prays for the Ephesians "that Christ may dwell *in your hearts* by faith; to the end that ye being rooted and grounded in LOVE, may be strong to apprehend with all the saints, what is the breadth, and length and height and depth, and to know the

Love of Christ, which passeth knowledge, that ye may be filled unto all the fulness of God'' (Eph. 3:17).

Before we go on to ask, not doubtingly, but in a spirit of joyous expectation, "*How* can these things be?" may we just answer the questions which are in the minds of some. "And *is* love *alone* really enough?" "Does 'love' indeed banish sin from my life?" "Does 'perfect love' mean 'holiness'?"

To answer such questions, we need only just look at that wonderful 13th chapter of 1 Corinthians in order to realize what Divine Love can work in us.

"Love suffereth long" — it drives away all impatience.

"Love is kind" — it leaves room for no unkindness.

"Love envieth not" — all jealousy is banished.

"Love vaunteth not itself" — boasting and self-assertion disappear.

"Is not puffed-up" — pride finds no place in the heart.

"Does not behave itself unseemly" — folly goes.

"Seeketh not its own" — "self" is dead — selfishness will be unknown.

"Is not provoked" — anger and wrath will not be seen.

"Taketh no account of evil" — brooding over so-called "wrongs" will be no more. Malice and all uncharitableness are not found in the heart.

"Beareth all things" — complainings will never be heard.

"Believeth all things" — mistrust will not destroy fellowship.

"Hopeth all things" — despair, anxiety, despondency go.

"Love never faileth."

No wonder Paul adds, "When that which is Perfect is come. . . . " What *is* it that is "Perfect"? — why, just the love of God — shed abroad in our hearts.

If "perfect love" casts out this great procession of sins, and fills our entire being, we might well cry out in an ecstasy of thankfulness and delight, "To me to live IS Christ" — and Christ is love. If we have not done so before, we must surely set ourselves the task of finding out how this great Possession can be secured.

How can we get this Perfect Love — and keep it?

Chapter IV

HOW SIN IS OVERCOME

Sin Is Overcome Only by the Indwelling Christ

We have now been led into a very definite position in Christian experience. It cannot be doubted that the Bible commands and expects some kind of "perfection," some kind of "holiness," without which no man can see the Lord.

But we long to see Him. We long to know, not only about Him, but to know HIM. This holiness cannot possibly be reached by man by his own efforts — no, nor by a man merely "helped" by God. "All our righteousnesses are as filthy rags" (Isa. 64:6).

But we have seen that Jesus Christ has promised to come and make His abode in our hearts: bringing His own "perfect love" and pure holiness into our very being.

When "HE is our LIFE," then we indeed know HIM. "And this is life eternal, that they might know Thee, the only true God, and Jesus Christ Whom Thou has sent" (John 17:3). And Jesus Christ is "perfect love." And perfect love casteth out, not only fear, but all sin.

All this we have seen — perhaps for many years. Now it is easy enough to write such things, and — in some sort of way — believe such things. But we want more than that. The question is, "How can I, a struggling sinner, though saved by grace, get this 'perfect love'? How can I get victory over all known sin, and live the Victorious Life?"

What God Can Do

God gives great and open sinners instant victory over great and open sins, and rescues such men from the clutches of such sins. We want to know how *we* can get instantaneous deliverance from little sins (so-called). The Loving Saviour and Almighty Redeemer CAN do it, we know — *but* how is it done?

This is the most momentous question any Christian man can ask. Most Christians have made many and frequent attempts to get victory over sin: and most of them have failed in the attempt. The great majority of believers reach a certain level in Christian experience, and then gradually slip back to lower levels. Why is this? Is it not probably because their method of attempt was wrong?

This is such an important matter that we hope the reader will patiently examine the following criticisms. We say "patiently," because so much will be said which cuts right across the usual advice given to seekers after sanctification. The writer knows full well what he is talking about. He has himself sadly trodden all the paths described, and has tasted both their joys and their sorrows. And today as he looks back, he realizes why they failed to lead him into the Victorious Life.

The Popular Way

Fight your temptations. You have accepted Jesus Christ as your personal Saviour, yet you find your sinful passions still remain, and often break out into actual sin. You want victory over those temptations, for tempted we always shall be here on earth. Very well — make a victorious struggle (by God's help, of course) against these evil passions and desires, and in this way overcome them.

This idea appeals to us, and seems so good and wise.

Chapter V

NONE CAN IMITATE CHRIST

*Not the Imitation of Christ But His
Indwelling Presence Is the Real
Secret of Constant Triumph*

Have we grasped the fact that the Victorious Life is not secured *gradually,* nor by effort and striving on our part? We know that a partial self-control can be obtained and *is* obtained for a time by men who give no thought to pleasing God. An athlete will "flee youthful lusts" and to a great degree "keep himself unspotted from the world" simply to gain Victory in the world of sport. A businessman or a shop-assistant will "control" his temper merely to secure orders, or keep a situation. A society lady will remain "sweet" even if you ruin her smartest dress by upsetting your tea over it. A Christian man may "school" himself in the same manner — but this is not necessarily the Victorious Life.

Do not misunderstand me. There *is* a fight — and a strenuous fight — against a world of sin. But to fight against sin *in the heart* is to mistrust Christ and is sure of failure in the long run. What then *can* we do to get this Victorious

Life? Many of us have tried the *Imitation of Christ.*
We may call this

The Promising Way

because it looks so attractive and right; and so likely to
succeed. Surely it is a splendid thing to imitate Christ. But
can you do it? "Oh, well," you reply, "I can try." As a
matter of fact, no one ever lived who imitated Christ. It
cannot be done. Nor are we told to attempt it.

Christ Our Life

One of the world's masterpieces of religious literature is
called *The Imitation of Christ.* Most of us know it well. It is,
indeed, a delightful book, and has helped countless
thousands — but not to imitate Christ! John Newton, the
blaspheming slave raider, was led to Christ by reading this
book. Read it again, for your soul's good, and you will notice
that from beginning to end there is nothing about imitating
Christ. It is full of helpful counsels and advice, of medita-
tions, and prayers and exhortations. The title well might be
The Appropriation of Christ, or *The Absorption of Christ.*

Christ is to be more than an example — He is *our life.*
Someone has gone so far as to have declared that the "idea of
imitating Christ is a hoax of the devil"! And he is really right
in his strong assertion. For although no harm, but only good,
can come from attempting to imitate the Lord Jesus, failure is
certain to be the result. Good is always the enemy of "best."
We know how hopeless it is to try to imitate the holy men and
women whose friendship we value. How much more difficult
it would be to imitate Christ!

The Bible on Imitators

But we must not rely upon human opinions. What does
the Bible say about this question? Has it ever struck you that
nowhere in the New Testament are we told to be like Jesus
Christ — or to strive to be like Him — or to pray that we may
be like Him? Is it not so? This is very startling. The nearest
approach you get to such an idea is found in Romans 8:29,

Chapter VI

HOW TO ENTER IN

*How to Be Wholly Possessed by Christ and
Thus Enter Into and Enjoy the
Life of Holiness*

If, then, we are unable to become holy by struggling against our sins; and if we cannot imitate Christ so as to become like Him, what hope is left us?

Hope? The writer soon discovered that there was not only no hope, but miserable failure in struggling and trying to "imitate."

The Quest for God's Presence

But there came a bright star on his spiritual horizon. It was hailed with all the joy of the wise men of old when they "saw the star." Surely this wondrous light would lead him into the very presence of the Lord — and there he would find victory? A little book was given him by a fellow-worker. It was called *The Practice of the Presence of God,* by Brother Lawrence. It made a profound impression on his life.

Brother Lawrence found that books of devotion and religious "exercises" did not help him — but were rather hindrances to his spiritual life, so he set himself to work to secure at all times a sense of God's presence. He endeavoured always to walk as in the presence of God. The result was a communion with God so close and uninterrupted that set times of prayer were not different from other times. "The time of business," said he, "does not with me differ from the time of prayer; and in the noise and clatter of my kitchen, while several persons are at the same time calling for different things, I POSSESS GOD in as great tranquillity as if I were on my knees at the Blessed Sacrament."

Now, is not that the spirit we want? "In Thy presence is fullness of joy," says the Psalmist (Ps. 16:11). But is this the Victorious Life? It certainly seemed so to Brother Lawrence.

The booklet was inspiring. Never before had the writer experienced such a wonderful uplift of soul: such an inspiration for service.

Not only the knowledge that "Thou, God, seest me," but the habitual consciousness, "I am now in the very presence of God." The mind went back to Zacharias in the Temple and the words of the Archangel, "I am Gabriel, that stand in the presence of God" (Luke 1:19). Ah! that's the thought. His feet may tread the temple courts, but he never forgets that he stands in the very presence of God. "Take heed," said the Lord Jesus Christ, "that ye despise not one of these little ones . . . for their angels do always BEHOLD THE FACE OF MY FATHER which is in heaven."

In the Presence of God

That, then, is the secret of the angels' service — they are always conscious of being in the presence of God. Was it not so with Elijah? When he suddenly emerges from obscurity and springs into our view he cries, "As the Lord God of Israel liveth before Whom I STAND!" (1 Kings 17:1; 18:5). When he refused "to stand" in the presence of God, he begged that he might die; and God could not use him again till he "stood" once more in His presence. "Go forth," said God to the despondent prophet, "and STAND upon the mount before the Lord" (1 Kings 19:11). But he hid in the cave.

Then came wind, and earthquake and fire — but all in vain. They did not drive him forth from his hiding-place from God. After the fire there was a sound of gentle stillness (v. 12, R.V., marg.). Did the prophet fear that God had deserted him? Had God departed? Elijah wrapped his face in his mantle and went out and STOOD in the entering in of the cave. Once more he "stands" before God, and God could speak to him and use him.

Yes. All this is Scriptural. Oh, what resources of help and strength and comfort lie in this thought, "I . . . stand in the presence of God." When some unwelcome duty, some unpleasant task, or some "big thing" had to be faced the writer has again and again steadied himself, nerved himself by quietly repeating the words, "I . . . stand in the presence of God."

What Our Lord Desires

We thank God with unfeigned gratitude for this help by the way. But it is not the Victorious Life. A *heathen* may use such help.

During the war a troopship was torpedoed in the Mediterranean and was fast sinking. A British soldier in great terror hurried hither and thither bewildered. A Hindu put his hand on the shoulder of the terrified man and pointing upward said, "Johnnie" (their equivalent of Tommy); "God!" And this steadied the lad. Helpful; but not sufficient. It may be the source of strength for angels, and for saints *before the day of Pentecost*. But we need something more than this.

And the Lord Jesus has promised us this "something more."

Is, then, the Way of the Presence right or wrong? Surely it is right as far as it goes. No one will ever know what a help the writer found it. After all, we are "IN Christ" and to remind ourselves of His presence around us — near us — must be helpful.

The Christ Dwelling Within

But our Lord's great desire is that we shall realize His presence within us. He tried to get His disciples to believe (and to know) that the Father was in Him and He in the Father (John 10:38). That He could do nothing of Himself — but that the Father was working in and through Him (John 5:19,30). And that in the same way we are sent by Him. That without Christ we can do nothing — but He would come and dwell IN us and work in and through us. Christ Jesus says this with the utmost plainness.

"As Thou hast sent Me into the world," says our Lord in His prayer, "even so have I also sent them" — the apostles (John 17:18). "At that day," (Pentecost) said Christ, "Ye shall KNOW that I am in My Father, and ye in Me, and I IN YOU" (John 14:20).

How can we get this Indwelling of Christ? And how know we have Him and thus "know Him and the power of His Resurrection"? How did Brother Lawrence get his blessing? How did he keep it? He just surrendered himself entirely to God. Without such surrender one cannot really practice the presence of God. "I know," said he, "that for the right practice of it, the heart must be empty of all other things; because God will possess the heart ALONE. And as He cannot possess it alone without emptying it of all besides, so neither can He act there and do in it what he pleases unless it be left vacant to Him."

This was his Prayer: "My God, here I am, all devoted to Thee. Lord, make me according to Thy heart."

And what was the result? He had such a joy in God that for 30 years his soul was so elated and exultant that he had to repress his raptures so as to hinder them appearing outwardly.

"Were I a preacher," he used to say, "I should above all other things preach the practice of the presence of God: so necessary do I think it and so easy too."

But one does not fully appropriate that life merely by accepting Christ as the Saviour from the guilt of sin. Many sincere Christians are living defeated lives. Their sinful passions — yes, and sinful desires — are not entirely gone. So there is failure, and such lives are little different from those of the worldlings around them.

There must be an entire surrender of self — a real yearning desire to be free from all known sin: a looking to Jesus Christ by faith to destroy sin in us; and a taking of Christ to be our whole life — literally our life.

"You will never have the Victorious Life," said Wilbur Chapman, "until Jesus Christ has all there is of you — never!" When He comes and takes entire possession of our being, He brings the Victorious Life, and we can say, "I live, and yet no longer I, but Christ liveth in me."

When He possesses us wholly, then we shall be holy. Are we willing to take the step? Are we willing to put ourselves unreservedly into His hands?

To do so is to secure Heaven on earth!

CHAPTER VII

BURIED WITH CHRIST

What it Means to be Baptized Into
Christ Jesus

"One of the bitterest moments of my life," said a missionary recently, "was when an earnest young Buddhist boy said to me, 'I want to believe in Christ, but I have never seen Him in those who profess Him. How can I believe in someone Whom I have not seen?'"

Would that lad have spoken in the same way had he known us? At all costs we must have the fullness of the Indwelling Christ.

The Holy Spirit's Chief Work

The chief work of the Holy Spirit is to reveal Christ. How often we have prayed, "O God fill us with Thy Holy Spirit." We hear the prayer again and again at prayer meetings with little apparent result. Why is it? Is God to blame? Are *we* to blame?

"He shall glorify ME," said Christ, "for He shall receive of Mine and show it unto you." So then it is the work of the Holy Spirit to see that Christ is "formed within" us

(Gal. 4:19). If then God answers our prayer and fills us with His Holy Spirit, we shall indeed be wonderfully conscious of the indwelling Christ. So will others be!

Now let the writer confess that he has often spoken about this doctrine and has read the Gospel and Epistle of St. John again and again without really appropriating this indwelling of Christ. The Lord Jesus has been within the heart for many years, "for if any have not the Spirit of Christ, he is none of His" (Rom. 8:9). But the Lord Jesus was not filling the *whole* heart. There must be many believers in a like condition. Many have told me by letter and lip how they have agonized for this Victorious Life for 20, 30, even 40 years, without getting it. "For years I have agonized for this," wrote a clergyman to me. "What a difference it would make to my ministry! What a blessing it would prove to my people! Tell me how I can get it." How then can this fullness of blessing be secured? Only by letting Jesus Christ do what all our strugglings and strivings have failed to do.

We cannot overcome any sin by *trying* to do so. Christ only has conquered sin. He conquered it not for Himself — the devil had nothing in Him. He conquered it for you — for me! He doesn't ask me to do what He has already done. He *does* ask me to enter into His victory. We cannot grow by trying to grow. We cannot grow in grace by trying to grow in grace. It is all of Christ. How?

A Divine Secret Revealed

St. Paul says that there was a great secret hidden from age to age, but which it pleased God to reveal to him. What is it? "Christ IN YOU the hope of glory" (Col. 1:27). "God was pleased to make known what is the riches of the glory of this mystery" — that He "may present every man perfect in Christ Jesus" (Col. 1:28). Heathen religions have tried to bring their gods down to man — with the passions and vices of humanity! Our Lord came Himself and lived as a man: Emmanuel, "God with us!" Isn't it a stupendous thought that the high and lofty One that inhabiteth eternity, Whose Name is HOLY, should dwell not only in the high and holy place but also "with him that is of a contrite and humble spirit — to revive [give new life to] the humble" (Isa. 57:15)? Christ came to take us into Himself, and He Himself comes into us. He the Head; we His body. He the Vine; we the branches. Thus His life is IN US.

This is the "overcoming life," the life more abundant, the Victorious Life. How do Christians come to understand how to enter in? Many, like the writer himself, found the "secret" entrance through careful and prayerful study of Romans 6:3-11. "Are ye ignorant that all we who are baptized into Christ Jesus . . .?" What is it to be baptized into Christ Jesus? Again and again Paul reminds believers that they are "in Christ" — that they have "put on Christ." When does this happen? It takes place the moment a man, woman or child accepts Jesus Christ as Saviour. Baptism is a rite ordained by Christ which expresses baptism into Jesus Christ.

When Christ Is Received

The new life — the life from above, the regenerate life — is a miraculous life, and it is the result of our being taken into Christ. The instant we received Christ as Saviour we were made part of Him. In Paul's day, a man was apparently baptized immediately he believed in Christ. So Paul takes baptism to illustrate or even prove the fact that a believer is taken into Christ. We are made "members" of Christ — a part of His body. So that Christ's life becomes our life, and we can say, "Christ Who is our life" (Col. 3:4). Get hold of this truth.

An old lady who, late in life, accepted Christ as her Saviour, was always praising God and talking about her Saviour. One day a friend said, "You seem pretty confident about this Saviour of yours! I wouldn't be too sure about it, if I were you. Suppose the Lord should let you slip through His fingers?" "But," said the old lady, "I'm one of His fingers." Now she was perfectly right — she was indeed a member of Christ. We dare not say such a thing if it were not openly told us in Scripture.

It is all too wonderful for words. I, a poor sinner saved by grace, have been made a member of the Lord Jesus Christ Himself.

"I hope," said a critic of an address on this subject by the writer, "I hope the speaker is not making out that we are all little gods!" Far from it. But we do "make out" that we have a great God living in us and making us members of Himself.

Baptized Into Christ

"Are ye ignorant that all we who were baptized into Christ Jesus were baptized into His death?" Are we "ignorant" as to what this means? Here, again, the writer must plead guilty of failing for years to grasp the import of these words.

"In Adam all die" — yes, we are conscious enough of that — "who is a figure of Him that was to come" (Rom. 5:14). This surely means that we must in some way share the death of Christ? Every believer went to death with Christ on the Cross. "I have been crucified with Christ," says Paul.

"We were buried, therefore, with Him through baptism into death" (Rom. 6:4). St. Paul is thinking of baptism by immersion. This is a symbol of burial (which means *a previous death*). As the believer went right under the water, he realized that he was dead and buried. Dead as regards the old life — dead to sin. Sin has no power over a dead man. No "dominion" over him. "For he that is dead is freed from sin . . . . Reckon ye yourselves to be dead indeed unto sin . . . Sin shall not have dominion over you" (Rom. 6:7).

But death could not "hold" Christ, nor can it hold us, if we are in Christ. After death and burial — what? "That like as Christ was raised from the dead through the glory of the Father, so we also might walk in newness of life" (Rom. 6:4). Jesus Christ did not raise Himself: God raised Him. Over and over again we are told this: God raised Him from the dead. And all the mighty power which God exercised in raising Christ from the dead is at our disposal. And to think that we should for a moment imagine that our feeble struggles are also needed!

St. Paul longed that believers in his day should realize this. He prays for them that "having the eyes of your heart enlightened, ye may know what is the hope of His calling, what the riches of the glory of His inheritance in the saints, and what the exceeding greatness of His POWER TO US-WARD who believe." What power? "According to the working of the strength of His might which He wrought in Christ when He raised Him from the dead" (Eph. 1:18). THAT POWER GOD OFFERS YOU.

A Gift to Be Taken

Isn't it wonderful? Can we grasp it? Paul, seeing the stupendous nature of this gift, cries, "I count all things but refuse, that I may gain Christ: . . . that I may know Him, and the power of His resurrection" (Phil. 3:8,10). This mighty power in Christ is a gift to be "gained" by the removal of all hindrances.

How can we "know Him and the power of His resurrection"? Simply by being buried with Christ — being dead unto sin. That is, not only claiming forgiveness of our sins, but by God's help renouncing the world, the flesh and the devil — by forsaking all sin — and then looking to God in faith to raise us up to walk in newness of life.

Try to understand what death and resurrection meant to our Lord. There He is perfect God and perfect man nailed to the Cross. The sins of the world came upon Him. God cannot die, nor can He remain in contact with sin. So the Spirit of God in the perfect man "Jesus" forsook that body of clay. "He gave up the Ghost." And a dead *man* hangs upon the Cross. That perfect body is buried; and on the third day God raised Him from the dead. What happened? The Spirit of Christ came back into that dead human body and Christ Jesus rose again — once more perfect God and perfect man.

That is what God wishes to do for every man. When we can indeed "reckon ourselves to be dead unto sin" and "buried with Him by baptism into death"; then we can look to Christ *to put His Spirit into us* and to raise us up "to walk in newness of life." Then "our life" is no longer ours but is the Christ-Life. Not an imitation of Christ, but Christ Himself dwelling in our hearts by faith. Then we can humbly say with Paul, "I have been crucified with Christ, yet I live, and yet no longer I, but Christ liveth in me" (Gal. 2:20).

What a glorious privilege! What a tremendous responsibility! "It pleased God to reveal His Son IN me!" (Gal. 1:16).

When Self Is Dead

Is all this difficult to understand? It is all there on the page of Scripture. But praise be to God, it is not necessary for us to understand *how* God works — but just to believe that He will (and does) perform this work in us.

The question is just this: Am I willing to give up all known sin and to put myself absolutely at the disposal of the Saviour? — myself, my talents, my possessions, my work, my future? Am I willing to surrender myself entirely to Him? Dr. Wilbur Chapman for some time hesitated to trust his future career to Christ, although he was then a noted missioner. Dr. Meyer said, "Are you willing to be made willing?" Dr. Chapman told Christ he was *willing to be made willing*. At once every difficulty was removed. Yes, we must even surrender our surrender to Christ. Our Lord did not crucify Himself — nor bury Himself — nor can we crucify ourselves. But when we have emptied ourselves of "self," Christ will crucify us — and will "raise us up to walk in newness of life." The Cross for you and me is just I (self) crossed out.

The surrender must be absolute and entire. You remember the story of the goddess who, wishing to make her child Achilles immortal, dipped him beneath the waters of the river Styx. She succeeded with the exception of his ankles, by which she held him, thus preventing the water from laving that spot. His ankles were vulnerable and there he became mortally wounded. That fable has a moral truth.

There must be no part of us left unsurrendered in our burial with Christ through baptism unto death.

When Satan sees a man accept Christ as his Saviour, he tries his level best to keep his hand upon some small part of him. He wants to have just a *little* control over us, so that he can bring about our downfall. He knows that if he can prevent full surrender, he will also prevent a Victorious Life.

How to Be Filled

A man "full of the Holy Spirit" is a mighty power — which power almost vanishes when even a little of our surrender is withdrawn. That power is also impossible when a little of our surrender to Christ is withheld. But if with "full and glad surrender" we yield ourselves to our blessed Master, He will come and fill us wholly with His Divine Presence.

Can we trust our all to Him, so that He may become "all in all" to us? "Jesus Christ is the Saviour of *all* the life as well as the Saviour of every life."

CHAPTER VIII

SURRENDER ALL TO CHRIST

*What "Absolutely Surrendered to God" Really
Means, and the Results That Follow
This Attitude of Faith*

We have again and again declared that before anyone
can enter into the Victorious Life two things are necessary —
surrender and faith: man's part and God's part.

First of all, we must be willing to give up all known sin
and all self-will and surrender ourselves entirely into God's
hands. Then we must in faith look to God to sanctify us. So
the entrance in may be summed up in two simple mottoes: —

Let Go and Let God

Now it is extraordinary how difficult it is to make people
understand what "surrender" is. And when they *do* understand, it is still more difficult to persuade them that it is for
their good!

The writer sent a business letter to a Christian friend a
week ago and in it put this question: "May I ask if you are
entirely surrendered to Christ?" He called round the following day. He had just taken offense because of the conduct of a

51

fellow-Christian (who had been both courteous and right — but firm).

Irritation, censure and divergence from the truth were all exhibited in five minutes. Then as he left the room he turned and said in a surprised tone, "By the way, what did you mean by that hint in your letter that I am entirely surrendered to God? I *am* entirely surrendered to Him." It was quite obvious that he knew little about surrender. Yet he seemed perfectly satisfied with himself.

What Surrender Means

Many readers of this book may be equally satisfied. But many, we know, are yearning for a victory they do not possess, although they have sought it for many years. Will you examine your surrender? What does it mean? If we wish to be entirely yielded up to Christ we must leave three things with Him: the Past, the Future and the Present.

This involves the surrender of SELF — not merely of things. "Surrender your very selves unto God" (Rom. 6:13, Weymouth). A cleric in the U.S.A. once said, "Do you know that Campbell Morgan came to this country and preached one sermon that destroyed 40 years of my sermons. For 40 years I had been preaching on the duty of sacrifice — the denying things to ourselves; giving up this and that. We practiced it in our family. We would give up butter one week and try to use the money in some way that God might bless. Another week we would give up something else, and so on. Campbell Morgan said that what we needed to give up, was not things but *self:* and that was the only thing we had not given up in our home. We had given up everything under the sun, but self. We were giving up so many things that we had become proud of our humility!" So let us look at self. Am I willing to surrender it entirely to God, and just "Let go"?

There Is the Past

1. "But," you exclaim, "the past is dead and gone." Oh, no! Far from it. "The sins of the past are forgiven, but

oh, what a weight they are about our necks!'' said a worker for Christ. This ought not to be. Are we willing to let the past go?

A lady missionary who longed for Victory through Christ and confessed her deep yearning for it, was just broken-hearted over the matter. Why? ''Because of the sins of the past,'' she replied. ''But God has forgiven your past sins. They are blotted out. How can they hinder you?'' ''But you do not know the sort of failures I have made!'' she moaned. ''No — the past is too awful.''

When she had surrendered her past, the blessing came. There is a hymn which runs, ''When God forgives, He forgets.'' ''For I will be merciful to their iniquities and their sins will I remember no more'' (Heb. 8:12; 10:17). Why, then, should *I* remember my past sins? Surely no good can possibly come of it?

Things That Mar Service

A momentary recollection of what God has saved us from may add to our praise of Him. But haven't we enough to bless and praise His glorious name for, even without such backward glances? It is bad enough to have sinned in the past: but it is surely a terrible thing to allow past sins to mar present service.

When you have forgiven your child some wrongdoing, do you wish him to grieve over it — to be miserable over it for days, weeks, months, years? Yet many children of God are doing this. Self-examination has its place, but to wreck the present by mourning over the past is sin.

Look at Simon Peter. He denied our Lord with oaths and curses. Our Lord forgave him, reinstated him, and used him. The one of the eleven who fell the lowest was the very one chosen to be spokesman on the day of Pentecost. Nor did Peter allow his past fall to hamper him, for he accuses the Jews of the very sin he had himself committed.

''Ye denied Him,'' he cried. ''Ye denied the Holy One and the Just'' (Acts 3:14). O let us thank God that the sins of the past are blotted out, and let us never grieve Him by spoiling the present by reproaching ourselves for the sad past. "Looking unto Jesus" must be our attitude. "Forgetting the things that are behind; . . . I press on toward the prize of the high calling of God in Christ Jesus" (Phil. 3:13).

There Is the Future

2. Are we willing to leave that entirely in God's hands? Many people seem to think that God will take advantage of them! That if they agree to obey all God's wishes, God will make them miserable. They cannot trust God to fill their lives with joy — so they seek their pleasures from the world, and sometimes from deliberate sin.

The Lord Jesus said to His disciples, "These things have I spoken unto you that My joy might remain in you, and that your joy might be full" (John 15:11). What things had He been speaking about? Why, just abiding in Christ and keeping His commandments. His joy — the very joy of God!

Could we desire anything more than that — better than that? Of course, if He dwells in us, and lives His life in us, we have His joy.

From Tonight, Lord

A wayward little boy climbed onto his father's knees one evening and said, "Father, from tonight I'm going to do all you ask of me." How did the father act? Did he think to himself, "Now I have that boy in my power. Now I have the chance of making his life miserable!" It is unthinkable. He drew the laddie closer to him and silently vowed he would do everything in his power to make that boy happy.

Is a God of Love going to take advantage of us, if we surrender our all to Him? Will He deign to remain in our debt? Remember, God has not only the will, but the power to make us supremely happy. There are our future plans. Does not God know what is best for us? Yet how unwilling believers often are to trust Him to do what is best.

When addressing a party of missionaries home on furlough last summer, the writer was struck by the miserable face of an elderly man. "Why is he so miserable?" "Oh," replied the chairman, "he longs to return to China to die in harness, but the committee refuse to allow him to go back." A devoted servant of God — yet unwilling to leave his future in God's hands. The result was not fullness of joy — but misery. We might well pray, as one dear saint did, "Oh, God! do not let anyone here be afraid of Thee."

Are you afraid of God? Yes — if you know of anything you are not willing to give up, should God show you that it was His will you should do so.

> God knows, He loves, He cares;
> Nothing this truth can dim;
> He does the very best for those
> Who leave the choice to Him.

Then There Is the Present

3. How will this be affected? All unlove, bitterness, irritability, pride, jealousy, resentment, censoriousness — all must go, really go. An active lady worker said to the writer, "That's easy enough for me, for I haven't an enemy in the world!" The next day she was limping. "I've fallen down," she explained. "I saw that horrid Miss K—— coming along and I didn't want to acknowledge her, and in looking the other way, I slipped off the curb and fell in the gutter!"

Now we may be sure that if there is anyone against whom we harbor any ill-feeling or resentment, or "owe a grudge" — anyone to whom we could not show Christian love and kindliness — we are not living the Victorious Life. Dr. Schofield once said, "If you have a sin in your life which you cannot let go, bring it to Jesus and let Him kill it." It may be some habit which others regard as harmless.

"Whenever you talk of surrender," said a man to the writer, "I always think of my pipe." Not a word had been said about smoking — but the pipe went. Forgive this remark — it is true or it would not be recorded here: You will find very few fully surrendered Christians whose consciences allow them to smoke.

One word of warning. Do not allow any fear of the future to rob you of present victory. "I've surrendered all to Christ," said a missionary at Keswick last summer, "and I am so happy. But I'm fearful what will happen when I get home." Do you see, the future was not really surrendered.

Dr. A. T. Pierson in his last address at Mildmay said, "Believe me as a dying man, no one ever obtained as much as he might have obtained from God." Why? Because God cannot give all He would until we surrender all we have — and are. If you find any difficulty in this matter — then just surrender your surrender to the Lord Jesus.

Now Is the Day of Victory

The present is the time for Victory. Let your aim ever be to glorify the Lord Jesus now. So many Christians let present opportunities slip by unused, because their minds are fixed upon something they are going to do *tomorrow* or next Sunday. School yourself to live in the present. How can Christ Jesus manifest forth His glory — Himself through me today — now, this very moment?

Perhaps the secret of Victory in Christ lies just here. God gives needed grace just when it is needed.

"Have you dying grace?" asked a lady of Charles Spurgeon. "No, madam, and I do not want it now — but praise God, I have living grace," was his reply.

Surrender. Let go. Then look to Christ in faith. Let GOD ——.

Ask the Lord Jesus Christ to crucify you and to give you His Resurrection Life. In that delightful little book, *The Christian's Secret of a Happy Life,* there is a chapter on

"How to Enter In"

The way suggested is to pray, "Lord Jesus, I believe that Thou art able and willing to deliver me from all the care and unrest and sin of my Christian life. Thou didst die to set me free, not only in the future, but here and now. I believe that Thou art stronger than sin and canst keep me from yielding to it. Lord, I am going to trust Thee to keep me. I have tried keeping myself and have failed grievously. I am also helpless. So now I will trust Thee. I give myself to Thee. I keep nothing back. . . . And now I AM Thine.

"I believe that THOU dost accept this poor weak, foolish heart; and that it has been taken possession of by Thee; and that Thou hast at this moment begun to work in me to will and to do of Thy good pleasure. I trust Thee utterly, I trust Thee now."

But be careful to remember that surrender is not simply making a promise to God to forsake sin and always to do His will. That would be living under the Law. Surrender is just turning over to God all that we are and have, *for Him to do with us* whatever He wishes. Surrendered Christians are often defeated, because they think they can carry out their good resolutions by God's help. No! Just hand yourself over to God, and then trust Christ to do His part. "He is able to keep."

It is not our surrender that gives us the victory. It is not even our faith! It is CHRIST HIMSELF — the Faithful One.

Surrender and trust, and Christ will never fail you.

CHAPTER IX

REAL VICTORY AND FALSE — REAL VICTORY AND ITS COUNTERFEIT

The Victorious Life is simply a life fully surrendered to God, with Christ dwelling within and in complete control — a life in which the only desire is to bring glory to Jesus Christ. It is the only truly happy life, yet Christians refuse to enter in, lest their lives should be made miserable!

The Joy of Perfect Trust

But is it a life filled with ''crosses''? That is the idea that many Christians have — that where there is the choice between things agreeable and disagreeable, the unpleasant one must, of course, be chosen! Can we find anything of this in the Bible?

Paul is never tired of talking about the wonderful joy in his life. ''Rejoice evermore''; ''In everything give thanks.'' Yet what hardship and bitter persecution were his lot! If you love God and fully trust Him, the place in which you are is the happiest place in which you can possibly be; and the work you are doing is the very best for you. Of course, God may move you elsewhere or give you other work. That can be left to Him. But let Him be glorified in us NOW.

Crosses? Nowhere in the Bible do we read of crosses.

Yet when our plans are upset, or the weather "spoils" our day, or sickness or bereavement alters our prospects, we are apt to say sadly (or cheerfully), "Well, I suppose this is my cross for today." It may not be murmuring, but merely what we call "resignation." There should be no such word as "resignation" in the vocabulary of the Christian. If God has complete control over us, nothing can happen contrary to His will. And is not His will the very best for us? Instead of resignation there should be glad acceptance. The feeling of our hearts should ever be, "I delight to do Thy will, O my God!" (Ps. 40:8). There can be no such thing as disappointment in the life of a man really living the Victorious Life. "My meat is to do the will of Him that sent me," said our Lord (John 4:34). Can we say the same?

When we are transformed by the renewing of our mind we shall prove every day that God's will is good and perfect; shall it not therefore be acceptable? (Rom. 12:2). How eagerly, how joyfully we should embrace it! Believers are nowhere called upon to bear crosses.

Taking Up the Cross

We know, however, that Jesus Christ said: "If any man would come after Me, let him deny himself and take up his cross and follow me" (Matt. 16:24); "Whosoever does not bear his cross and come after Me cannot be My disciple" (Luke 14:27). It is, then, our duty to take up the cross, but not to carry crosses. There is one cross for every one and for every day.

If you had seen a man in our Lord's day carrying a cross you would know that it meant death to someone — probably for the man himself. The cross is always a sign of death. Before anyone can really follow Christ — really be a disciple, that is, a learner — he must be dead with Christ and risen with Him. That is what Paul meant when he said, "I have been crucified with Christ: yet I live, yet no longer I, but Christ liveth in me" (Gal. 2:20). Someone has said, "It is one thing to be saved from the penalty of sin; it is another thing to follow Christ."

Dr. Griffith Thomas says that some Christians are monstrosities. They are no more like Christ twenty years after their conversion than they were when they began the Christian life. They are not "learning" of Him. They have not taken up the cross: have not been crucified with Christ. "The taking up of the cross is the end of crosses and the beginning of discipleship," said Mr. C. G. Trumbull.

Do let us get hold of this fact: that our Lord wishes us always to be full of joy — always, everywhere, under all circumstances.

A gloomy, miserable-looking Christian stood outside a mission. "Will you come into our service tonight?" he asked of a passer-by. The stranger gave him one swift glance, and replied (as he hurried off), "No, thank you! I've troubles enough of my own!" Are we surprised?

A life of Victory is a life of Trust; and must be always full of Joy. Such a life glorifies Christ.

What Real Victory Means

But let us be quite clear as to what the Victorious Life is. For the devil does all he can to entice us to accept a counterfeit Victory — that is, a "victory" which we think we are getting ourselves by our own efforts.

Take the question of bad temper or irritability. Many Christians pride themselves on the fact that they exercise such self-control that their temper "never gets the better of them." By this they mean that they never *show* it. Now the Victorious Life is not one which merely makes our outward actions right. It is a life which gives victory in the inner realm of the heart, so that our very desires are right. To want to do wrongful things and to restrain from doing them is not real victory. The wonderful thing is that God takes the "want to" out of our very hearts, and we long only to do His will.

No doubt most of our readers have heard the story of the old Quaker lady who apparently never lost her temper. Under the most trying circumstances she was quite unruffled. A friend once commented on this, and said to her, "I cannot for the life of me understand how you always keep so delightfully sweet. Why, if the things happened to me which happen to you I should just boil over with rage; but *you* never do." The old Quaker lady quietly replied, "Perhaps I do not boil over, my dear, but thou dost not know what boiling is going on inside." Now that is not victory. There is no victory in keeping our sinful feelings from expressing themselves. We may do that simply because we are ashamed to let others know how sinful we are. Moreover, it does not require the grace of God to enable a man to hide his temper. A shop assistant in a drapery establishment will do that all day long — or he might lose his job. A businessman will do it to get an order. A "gentleman" will do it to avoid "bad form." A Society lady does it for social reasons. But this is not the Victorious Life.

When the Miracle Happens

An American speaker tells the following story to illustrate real victory. A lady missionary who had surrendered all to Christ but had never looked to Him for complete victory, found her temper not improved by the Tropics. She was much distressed about her failures, and her struggles against them seemed in vain. However, a friend showed her that there was victory through simple faith in Christ, and she claimed this victory as a gift of God. Writing to this friend some time afterwards she told of the wonderful thing that had happened in her spiritual life. "I wanted to write to you at first, but I was afraid it would not last," said she. "But it has lasted. Do you know that for three months not only have I not once slammed the door in the face of any of these stupid Indian servants that used to get on my nerves so, but *I have not even wanted to* — not once." Now that is victory.

We must recognize it as a miracle. No good resolutions, no will-power, can alter our likes and dislikes. But God can. He can take away from us all desire to do sinful things.

Bad temper is not the only sin of Christian people, and many Christians have the sweetest of dispositions. The best test of all is in the matter of love. Do we love our "enemies" — those who despitefully use us or persecute us? Do we nevertheless love them? "If you want him to love you, you must knock him down," said a worker to the writer, speaking about a friend. What is your first feeling when men injure you or oppose you? Is it a spontaneous outflowing of love towards them? Or do we first find it necessary to shoot up an urgent, earnest prayer that we *may* love them, and may not feel resentment? Do we eagerly welcome opposition, unkindness, rudeness, discourtesy (and suchlike) towards us, as opportunities of showing that the love of Christ is filling our hearts? It is in small matters we are tested.

Under the Love of Christ

How often we hear earnest Christian people saying, "I cannot love the unlovable." No; it is impossible for human love to do this. We cannot make ourselves love another. Human love is kindled only by what it thinks is lovable. The love of God — Christ's love — embraces all and sees everyone to be lovable. When Christ dwells richly in our hearts we shall love even our enemies. There is victory when "the love of God is shed abroad in our hearts" (Rom. 5:5), to the expulsion of all unlove — then and then only. There we have a definition of real victory.

Facts That Help Love

At first such a thing seems beyond our highest hopes. Many regard it as an impossibility. So it is to man. But with God this thing is possible. It is a miracle, and God works miracles every day. Fellow-Christian, do not give up the idea of living the Victorious Life because it seems impossible to you. Just yield yourself to Christ, and trust Him to work in you both to will and to do His good pleasure (Phil. 2:13).

Many reply that their faith is not strong enough. Why, faith the size of a grain of mustard seed is enough if you will exercise it. May we give you two FACTS to help your love and faith? Remember that: —

1. The Lord Jesus dearly loves all those whom we might regard as unlovable: loves them every bit as much as He loves us. Can we not see them with the eyes of Christ?

"Do not be afraid of me, mum," said a filthy, wild-looking tramp to a lady who crossed the road to avoid meeting him. "Do not be afraid of me, mum. My mother was a woman." Do not refuse to love me," the unlovable might exclaim. "The Lord Jesus LOVES ME."

2. The most unlovable person — the most loathsome and repulsive creature — becomes lovable even in *our* eyes when the love of God is shed abroad in HIS heart. If you really want to love him, pray earnestly for him and try to save his soul. If he is a Christian — but "nastily saved," as the Lancashire man put it — pray that he may get the Victorious Life; send him this book and continue in prayer. The writer has had the joy of pointing to Christ as their Savior most revolting men and women, in whom every vestige of beauty appeared to be stamped out by drunkenness and vice. He has met them a week after, new creatures in Christ Jesus. A miraculous transformation has taken place in an incredibly short time. Is he — she — unlovable in your eyes? Then just think what that one may become when the love of God reaches him or her.

Liberating the Angel

Michelangelo lingered before a rough block of marble so long that his companion remonstrated. In reply, Michelangelo said with enthusiasm, "There's an angel in that block and I'm going to liberate him!" Oh, what unbounding love would manifest itself in us towards the most unlovable — the most vile — if only we saw what they might become, and in our enthusiasm for souls we cried out, "There's the image of Christ — marred, scarred, well-nigh obliterated — in that dear fellow, and I'm going to make that man conscious of it."

A fable declares that a gallant prince kissed a serpent and it became a lovely princess. Fact shows us that when "kissed" by love the vilest may become beautiful; the "serpent" become a saint.

"What are the outward and visible signs of the Victorious Life?" asked a young evangelist of the writer. The answer to that question would describe real victory. Briefly we would say: Everything contrary to love is expelled from the heart and life. Read the closing words of Chapter III, and you will see what Divine LOVE can do — or rather, what LOVE DOES in scores and hundreds of lives. It drives out impatience, unkindness, jealousy, envy, boasting, self-assertion, pride, folly, selfishness, self-seeking, anger, irritability, bad temper, fretfulness, malice, uncharitable remarks, complaining, censoriousness, despair, anxiety, despondency, backbiting, repeating damaging information even if it is true. ALL THESE WE CALL RESPECTABLE SINS — or even refuse to regard them as sins at all! God help us! So long as any of these — even one of these — remains, there is no victory for us. When a fully surrendered Christian looks in simple faith to Christ and asks Him to fill the whole heart, HE, CHRIST, who is love, "perfect love," banishes every one of these vile "respectable" sins, which we have been regarding as LITTLE sins, but which mar our work and hinder our usefulness. Are we willing to allow the Lord Jesus to do this for us?

CHAPTER X

THIS LIFE IS A GIFT

*The Victorious Life Is All a Gift Received
in Faith and Is Not Obtained by Striving
and Struggling*

This Victorious Life is a *gift* and is not to be secured by any struggling or striving on our part. It is not a thing to be attained to by long and laborious effort. It is not a thing we can reach gradually by growing more and more like Christ. This must be clearly seen.

All life comes as a gift. Our physical life — we just receive it. Our spiritual life is "the gift of God" (Rom. 6:23). The life "more abundant" is a gift. We cannot receive a gift *gradually*. There may be hesitation or delay in taking it, there may be a struggle before we are willing to receive it. But a gift is accepted not gradually, but in a moment. It is obtained not attained.

The Victorious Life, then, can be received by a definite act. There is, of course, a "growth in grace" in the man who is wholly sanctified — a going on to perfection as his capacity increases.

But "this life is in His Son" (1 John 5:11). When we

67

accept the Son as the Lord of all our being, we receive (as a gift) the LIFE. It is something God does for us — IN US. There is, however, often a long struggle before surrender. Many a Christian has a terrific struggle before he is willing to yield himself wholly to Christ.

But this is before the Victorious Life begins. Victory begins only when struggling ceases. The moment you surrender yourself entirely to Christ and look to Him in faith to dwell in your entire heart that moment He comes and takes control of you.

Taking Christ at His Word

This indwelling is quite independent of any feeling on your part. It is independent of any ideas of your own as to how He should manifest His presence. You must just take Him at His word and rest upon that — not upon any feeling. You may feel a wonderful thrill of joy. You may feel nothing unusual. Can you trust His promise?

Every Christian has to decide whether he will be wholly consecrated to God, or whether he will remain content to live the Christian life on a low level — which is *always* a powerless one, and a perilous one.

The Crisis and the Process

This DECISION FOR HOLINESS is a crisis in a Christian's life. With it comes an instantaneous revelation of God to him, that Christ can be all in all; that Christ can and does give Victory over all known sin: not gradually but INSTANTANEOUSLY. "Having therefore these promises let us cleanse ourselves from all defilement of the flesh and spirit perfecting holiness in the fear of the Lord" (2 Cor. 7:1). The tense in the Greek shows that this is done at once as a definite and decisive act. This is the *crisis* of sanctification.

But after this definite steps of whole-hearted dedication of one's self to God, there comes a life-long process of sanctification — a going on from strength to strength, from glory to glory. A *process* under which the believer becomes more and more conformed to the life and character of Christ.

Where Many Blunder

We have dwelt long on this point because the mistake the writer made (and which many of his readers have probably made) was to try to experience the process without first experiencing the crisis of sanctification. There is little — if any — growth in grace until we have claimed by surrender and faith the "life that is Christ." Have you experienced the crisis? Have you obeyed the command, "Sanctify in your hearts Christ as Lord" (1 Peter 3:15)? Christ is in the heart of every believer as "JESUS" — Saviour. But is He indeed Lord? It is not a question of re-conversion, it is just a question of recognizing the indwelling Christ as Master in His own house — my heart.

Remember, however, that surrender alone, that is, "decision," is not enough. That is only our part in giving up all hindrances to blessing. If surrender sufficed, then we should make sanctification to be a mere act of the *will*. We are neither saved nor sanctified by what we give up, but by what we receive. It is "the very God of peace Who sanctifies us wholly." After surrendering ourselves, we must look to Christ to crucify us and to raise us from the death to sin to live the resurrection life.

Let go — surrender: then "let God" do His part. But God will not allow any effort or struggle on your part to help Him. Salvation is entirely a gift of God: entirely of grace.

Now salvation is a threefold work: Past, Present and Future. Justification, sanctification and glorification.

Eternal Life a Gift

And it is all by faith. You cannot earn, or get, any part of it by your own efforts or struggles. "For by grace have ye been saved through faith; and that not of yourselves: it is the gift of God: not of works, that no man should glory" (Eph. 2:8,9. See Rom. 11:6). Paul goes even further than this. "Ye are severed from Christ, ye who would be justified by the law" (*i.e.,* effort) (Gal. 5:4). When a man accepts Christ as a Saviour from the penalty of sin, he learns that Christ's forgiveness is absolutely and entirely through faith. Sorrow for sin, good resolutions, and tears, often accompany repentance. But repentance does not save a man. We have to leave that to Christ. Justification is entirely the work of Christ; and faith in Him secures this salvation. We can do nothing whatever to gain or merit it. We accept it as a gift.

When Christ shall come again, we shall be glorified. This is the future of salvation. In this work of glorification we know we can do absolutely nothing. It is all of Christ.

Life More Abundant — A Gift

What about the present? That is, our sanctification (which is first a crisis and then a process). We have called this the Victorious Life.

When we claim it by faith, there is the crisis. When we live it day by day, there is the process.

Our Blessed Saviour justified us, and will glorify us by His own power entirely. Does He need or demand our help in the matter of sanctification? How much will our struggling and striving or agonizing avail against the devil? Absolutely nothing. He is far stronger than we are. Does Christ, the Almighty Saviour, need my struggles to assist Him? Remember, our weakness will never be made strong. A dear Christian lady in an address on this subject said, "*Is* not the Christian life a long struggle? But thank God He gives us power to struggle!" Exactly the reverse is true. While we struggle, He cannot help us as He would, we limit and restrain His power.

The Victorious Life is simply salvation in the present; and all salvation is entirely of grace — entirely of Christ — a GIFT. "As therefore ye received Christ Jesus the Lord, *so* walk in Him" (Col. 2:6). How did we receive Him? By simple faith. How are we to walk in Him; that is, live a Victorious Life? By simple FAITH. "If we live by the Spirit (*i.e.,* eternal life is ours as a gift by the power of the Spirit), by the Spirit let us also walk" (Gal. 5:25). Do get hold of this truth: we may not, cannot in the smallest degree share with

Christ the work of accomplishing any part of our salvation. Yet so many of us imagine that in the matter of sanctification we must "paddle our own canoe."

Trust, Not Struggle

Blaze it out in letters of fire, that Christ can, and will, save us from the power of sin every day and every hour with our struggling, striving and agonizing. If you struggle, you do not trust.

Have not most of us learned from our own experience how useless our struggles are? Some besetting sin gets the better of us. How we struggle against it! How we agonize in prayer over it — even "standing on the promises of God" as we think. Yet we get up from our knees only to fall again and again into sin! Christ's promises cannot give us power. Even faith cannot save us. Only Jesus Christ can do it.

Are we willing to look to Him and trust Him to conquer our sin for us? He has conquered sin and Satan. HE — the Conqueror — is willing to come and fill our hearts and be OUR LIFE. "Sin shall NOT have dominion over you," says God's Word (Rom. 6:14). We may be "more than conquerors" — not by struggling, but entirely "through HIM that loved us" (Rom. 8:37). What does it mean? Not only that the besetting sin will be conquered — but the very *desire* to sin will be taken away.

Only Christ can do this. It is a wonderful *miracle*. Some of us have proved this.

A well-known character in London has recently passed to the life beyond the grave. He was a notorious drunkard, but marvellously saved by Christ. For weeks after his conversion he had an intense desire to drink coming upon him with almost overwhelming power. He fought and struggled against the temptation. Although an untutored man he felt that God had a better way than this. Kneeling in a field in North London he cried out, "O God, can't you make a better job of me than this?" And God at once took away all desire to drink and the craving never returned.

The saintly Bishop Moule confessed in an address to

confirmation candidates that a severe and terrible temptation assailed him in the street. He added, "I stopped dead and said quickly, 'Holy Spirit, come in.' Then I said to myself, 'The evil spirit, who is strong, is here. But I have the Holy Spirit, Who is Almighty, and I can leave Him to deal with the temptation.' "

Christ does not give us power apart from Himself. "All power is given unto Me" said Christ. "And lo! I am *with you* all the days" (Matt. 28:18,20).

"For if while we were yet enemies we were reconciled to God through the death of His Son, much more being reconciled shall we BE SAVED BY HIS LIFE" (Rom. 5:10) — *i.e.*, by the living Christ living in us. He will keep us safe from the power of sin, if we will let Him. Christ can do this. He will do it. He does it in every life that trusts Him to do it.

Self-Effort Means Failure

We have proved by our own experience that we cannot be good by self-effort. Stop trying to be good. Stop struggling, and let the Saviour do the great work for you. He came "to save His people from their sins" (Matt. 1:21). We can reckon on Him. "The promise is to him that worketh not, but believeth" (Rom. 4:5). "It is God that worketh in you both to will and to do" (Phil. 2:13).

"My God shall supply all your need according to His riches in glory in Christ Jesus" (Phil. 4:19). Dear Christian, is your most urgent NEED just deliverance from this awful sin? How you have struggled and agonized! Yet the supply is IN YOU!

"Ah," you cry, "but you do not know how weak I am." No — but we thank God for your weakness. "My grace is sufficient for you — for My POWER is made perfect in weakness" (2 Cor. 12:9). Your weakness, which has been your lament, shall be your highest glory.

"Most gladly therefore will I glory in my weakness, that the power of Christ may cover me" (2 Cor. 12:9). We can be kept *only* "by the power of God through faith"

(1 Peter 1:5). "Thanks be unto God which giveth us the Victory through our Lord Jesus Christ" (1 Cor. 15:57).

Pressing Towards the Goal

Does this mean, then, that we need do nothing but sit down and sing psalms? Far, far from it! We have been speaking only of the matter of our own personal salvation — past, present, future. ALL of this must be accepted as a gift. But when Christ comes into the heart, He comes with power. "Ye shall be endued with power [dynamite] from on high" (Luke 24:49). Power is a thing which makes itself felt. "Woe is unto me if I preach not the Gospel!" (1 Cor. 9:16) says Paul, whose teaching we have given above.

"We cannot but speak the things which we saw and heard" (Acts 4:20). Struggling and agonizing play no part in our personal salvation. They merely hinder and hamper it. But we are in the midst of a wicked generation. The devil is strongly entrenched in the lives of men and women around us. They encourage temptation and welcome it. They find their greatest enjoyment in sin. They do not want to conquer sin. So Paul, who declares that salvation is all of faith, also warns us that we have a fight to wage, a race to run, a wrestling to engage in. "The God of peace shall bruise Satan" says Paul: but "it is under OUR FEET" (Rom. 16:20). The enemy's Conqueror working in you will make the struggle short and decisive. He Who made peace FOR you, works peace IN you. All our powers of body, soul and mind are to be brought to bear upon this great task. In this "race" Paul presses on towards "the goal unto the prize of the upward calling of God in Christ Jesus" (Phil. 3:14). What *is* this prize? Certainly not forgiveness of sin, or power over temptation, or the gift of eternal life. The "runner" has already laid aside "every weight and sin" (Heb. 12:1), or he would not be in the race at all. No! The "prize" is not eternal life — that is a gift. The race, the fight, the wrestling (against the rulers of the darkness of this world — Eph. 6:12) is what we experience when we are fellow-workers of Christ, who came to destroy the works of the devil. (See Gal. 5:

19-21 for some of them.) Never forget that even in all this outward activity it is fruitful only as Christ inspires *it* and empowers *us*.

Our Lord's Example

Our Lord Himself "strove" in this way. He it was Who resisted unto blood, striving against sin (Heb. 12:4). But HE had not to struggle against any inward desire or any temptation to sin. HE did not find it hard to be good.

To sum up — there may be fierce conflicts in a Christian man's heart before he is willing to surrender himself entirely to Christ. And there *is* a great conflict to be waged against the devil, in our efforts to snatch others out of his bondage. But the Victorious Life, as it concerns our own souls, is one free from all struggle. "He is able to keep."

When the writer was a boy, he spent much time walking on stilts. He gained considerable freedom in their use. But although he "walked" it required constant effort, and sometimes struggle, to keep from falling. A little thing brought collapse. Contact with anyone usually meant a fall. That is a picture of the "walk" of many a Christian. Effort, struggle, slow progress, constant falls and new starts, and an almost total inability to help anyone else.

It is an unnatural "walk." Claim the Victorious Life — Victory through the Indwelling Christ — and the Christian walk will be found as easy as "walking on our feet."

Some shell-shocked soldiers with normal limbs believe they are unable to walk — and they cannot. The skillful physician makes them *believe* they can walk — and they do. The power of Christ to "walk by faith" is at our disposal. Can we not trust Him?

A little girl of 13 was asked what difference the Victorious Life meant to her in times of temptation? After a little pause she replied, "Before I saw this truth, I used to argue with the tempter, and he usually got the better of me. But now, when he knocks at the door of my heart, I say, 'Lord Jesus, will you answer the door for me?' And when Satan

74

sees the Lord Jesus within, he says, 'I'm sorry; I think I've come to the wrong house' — and he flees.''

How the Victory Comes

And what is true of our Victory over temptation through Christ alone is also true of the warfare we wage with the ''works of the devil'' around us. It is Christ — and not we ourselves — Who wins the Victory.

''What do you consider the most dangerous heresy of today?'' was a question asked of the Editor of the *Sunday School Times*. He passed by Christian Science, spiritism, higher criticism and other ''isms,'' and gave this answer: ''The most dangerous heresy is the emphasis that is being given by professing Christians on *what we do for God*, instead of on *what God does for us*.''

In our work for the Master let us remember that it is not we who are doing His work, but He Who is working through us.

This being so, every Christian who is living the Victorious Life will be much in prayer and in communion with God over the pages of His Holy Word.

Before we bring this chapter to a close we ought just to ask what effect the Victorious Life in us will have on others. So far, we have been dealing with ourselves. If we stopped there, we should still exclaim, ''It's worth having.'' But we are saved to serve. And every one of the many letters sent to the writer asking for help has come from Christians; from men and women trying to work for Christ, yet not equipped for service.

Dr. Temple, the new Bishop of Manchester, said at his enthronement, a few weeks ago, ''Remember that the converting power of the Church does not depend chiefly on the eloquence of its preachers, or the perfectness of its organization. It depends on the degree in which men see in the lives of Christians the evidence of the power of the love of Christ.'' That is it. And when men see that ''the love of Christ shed abroad in our hearts'' has such power that it has killed those sins in us which were so distressing to our friends, then they begin to think.

Love, the Conqueror

No one is beyond the reach of love. The power of Divine Love is infinite. In the days of the American war, there lived at Ephrata, a plain Baptist minister, Peter Miller, who enjoyed the friendship of Washington. There also dwelt in that town one Michael Wittman, an evil-minded man who did all in his power to abuse and oppose that minister. But Michael Wittman was involved in treason and was arrested, and sentenced to death. The old preacher started out on foot and walked the whole seventy miles to Philadelphia that he might plead for that man's life! He was admitted into Washington's presence and begged the life of the traitor. "No, Peter," said Washington, "I cannot grant you the life of your friend." "My friend!" exclaimed the preacher, "he is the bitterest enemy I have!" "What?" cried Washington. "You have walked seventy miles to save the life of an enemy? That puts the matter in a different light. I will grant the pardon." And he did. And Peter Miller took Michael Wittman from the very shadow of death, back to his own home in Ephrata — but he went no longer as an enemy but as a friend. And so it came to pass that love brought a reviler from the foot of the gallows to the foot of the cross.

Christian worker, listen! Are you getting the success you would like to see in your work for Christ? Are you getting *any* apparent success? If not, is it not worthwhile — for your own sake, for your work's sake, for the Saviour's sake, for lost sinners' sake — to enter the life of Victory?

Surrender: Faith: Taking: Praising the Giver.

.

CHAPTER XI

NOT SINLESS PERFECTION

*How the Devil Uses the Bogey of "Sinless
Perfection" to Scare Away Many Sincere
Souls From Seeking a Life of Holiness*

Have we really grasped the fact that the Victorious Life is a gift from God? We may think of it as "the fullness of the Holy Spirit"; or we may think of it as Jesus Christ dwelling in the heart. Personally the writer finds the greatest help from the fact of the indwelling Christ, and the consciousness of this indwelling.

After all, the Holy Spirit's chief work is to take of the things of Christ, and show them to us.

How to Get a Gift

But however we may regard it, the Victorious Life is a gift. "If ye being evil know how to give good gifts to your children, how much more shall your Heavenly Father give the Holy Spirit to them that ask Him?"

"If thou knewest the gift of God," said our Lord to a sinful woman, "and Who it is that saith to thee, 'Give Me to drink,' thou wouldest have asked of Him and He would have given thee living water" (John 4:10).

Now what must I do to secure a gift? Just take it. If a gift is offered me for the asking, will it please the giver if, instead of taking the gift, I spend long weeks, or months, or years begging and praying and agonizing for it?

Would it give pleasure to a father and mother if their children sat up all night agonizing in prayer for the Christmas gift they had promised to give them?

If they did such a thing their "agonizing" would have absolutely nothing to do with their receiving the gifts. One could well imagine the distressed father telling his children that if they didn't cease their petitions and get to bed and trust him they should get no gifts at all!

Jesus Christ is the great Christmas Day Gift. "Thanks be unto God for His unspeakable gift" (2 Cor. 9:15). That gift is ours. Someone has said, "Our Lord wants our lives on earth to be one long Christmas Day of receiving His gift of Himself as our victory."

We do not need to "agonize" about it; we do not need to work for it. Provided we are wholly surrendered to God we have simply to "receive," "take" the Gift of Christ Himself.

But did not Jesus Christ tell His disciples "to tarry in Jerusalem until they were endued with power from on high"? Yes, He did. "Wait," saith He, "for the promise of the Father."

But that was before Pentecost.

Ready for Our Acceptance

We never hear of the disciples after Pentecost telling believers to "wait" for this gift. In fact, we read in the 10th chapter of the Acts that the gift of the Holy Ghost fell upon "all them that heard the word," while St. Peter was yet speaking to the household of Cornelius, although none of them was yet baptized. The Holy Spirit was given to Gentiles without delay, on simple faith in Jesus Christ. There is no need today to wait at all. If we fulfill the conditions we can claim the gift.

The earliest disciples did not at first appreciate the value and necessity of this gift. Our Lord seems to have told ''more than 500 brethren'' to ''tarry until they were endued with power from on high.'' Yet only 120 obeyed the command, and consequently only 120 received the gifts on the day of Pentecost — the gift meant for all.

Let us today make no mistake about this. Our Lord is longing to fill every believer with His Holy Spirit. Christ is desirous of dwelling in our entire hearts by faith. Not until we have surrendered our wills to Him and have yielded our bodies to Him as well as our souls can He fill us with Himself.

This is what St. Paul means when he prays ''that He would grant you to be strengthened by His Spirit with power penetrating to your inmost being'' (Eph. 3:16, Weymouth). ''That ye may be filled unto all the fulness of God'' (Eph. 3:19), ''till we all attain unto the measure . . . of the fulness of Christ'' (4:13), ''the fulness of Him that filleth all in all'' (1:23).

Christ in His Fullness

It is very wonderful that He should be willing to come. But it is a glorious thing that He should be willing to take absolute responsibility in our lives, because He cannot make a mistake, and He cannot fail.

It seems incredible that any believer should refuse such a gift. Again we urge you — receive Him in His fullness by faith. Do not wait for or expect any ''thrill,'' any ''ecstasy.'' You may feel one, and you may not. But take Christ at His word, and believe that He has come into your heart to be your life. Then rely upon Him to supply all your need.

''Behold I stand at the door and knock; if any man hear My voice and open the door I will come in to him'' (Rev. 3:20).

Bear in mind that Christ is already in the heart of every believer — even in the heart of one who is only following afar off. But in so many cases He is not filling the *whole* heart. He has only partial possession; He has not complete control. There are often chambers of the heart which are shut against

Him. And not only closed, but with a lodger within, and that lodger a burglar waiting his time to gain entrance to other rooms within. "If any man . . . open the door."

We Christians sometimes sing:

> O Jesus, Thou art standing
> Outside the fast closed door,
> In lowly patience waiting
> To pass the threshold o'er:
> Shame on us, CHRISTIAN brothers,
> His name and sign who bear:
> Oh, shame — thrice shame upon us,
> To keep Him standing there.

And with the great majority of believers this is true of some part of the heart.

But it isn't so much the "shame" as the utter folly of it. For we know that He wishes to gain access to the whole of our hearts simply to bring richest blessing.

Paul implores the Roman Christians, "Yield yourselves unto God." He himself did so, and "heard His voice," with no closed door between — words unutterable; he felt joy unspeakable and full of glory, and in the fullness of his heart he cries, "Thanks be unto God for His unspeakable gift."

Temptation and Failure

"Is it possible to lose the Victorious Life?" is a question often asked. Indeed it is possible. Temptation will certainly come, and failure may occur. A great Christian leader of men told the writer, a few days ago, how he had sometimes temporarily lost the victory. "But," said he, "whenever I've failed, it has always been through the sin of worrying." Yet there *need* be no failure. We have a perfect Saviour. When we look back upon a break in this wonderful communion with Christ we shall always have to confess that the failure need not have occurred.

Sinless Perfection?

There are many saintly souls who openly declare that they never sin. They claim sinless perfection. They also claim that St. John teaches such a thing.

"We know that whosoever is begotten of God sinneth not, but He that was begotten of God (*i.e.,* Jesus Christ) keepeth him, and the evil one toucheth him not" (1 John 5:18). "Whosoever is begotten of God doeth no sin, because His seed (Jesus Christ) abideth in Him, and he cannot sin, because he is begotten of God" (1 John 3:9).

These statements refer not to single acts of sin, but to habitual sin. The tense used in the Greek does not imply that he cannot commit one definite act of sin, but that he cannot continue sinning; he cannot make a practice of sinning, or frequently repeat acts of sin; it is not his habit to sin. John is here speaking of known and voluntary sins, not of sins of infirmity or the falling short of the glory of God.

Tendency or Possibility

Any man can sin. Any man can tell a lie. But we know what we mean when we say "An honest man cannot lie." We do not accuse George Washington of untruth when he declared "I cannot tell a lie!"

Every sin is against a good man's nature. We say the "wood cannot sink." This is true. The tendency of wood is always to float. Yet there is always the possibility of its sinking. The hand of a child may submerge it; when sodden with water it will lie on the bottom. When the child releases it, it floats again. When a man is living the victorious life — a life maintained and actually lived for him by the indwelling Christ — there is no tendency to sin. He desires always to do those things which are pleasing to God. But there is always the awful possibility of his sinning. He may become absorbed in the "world;" he may allow temptation to gain entrance and the hand of Satan upon him may drag him down. So long, however, as a man is fully surrendered to Christ and in full communion with Him he cannot sin. But such a life is a moment by moment victory through a moment by moment faith. At any time he can partially withdraw his surrender or break his communion.

In the Father's Hands

A railway coach attached to a moving locomotive cannot stop. But at any moment the coupling may break and a stoppage ensue. Let us, however, repeat the statement that no man need commit any known and voluntary sin. "He is able to keep (guard) that which I have committed unto Him." The marginal reading is, "He is able to guard that which He hath committed unto me" (2 Tim. 1:12).

Both statements are true — praise be to God. "He is able to keep you from stumbling" (Jude 24).

Moreover our Lord Himself says of His followers, "No man shall snatch them out of My hand" . . . "And no one is able to snatch them out of the Father's hand" (John 10:28,29). And it is evident that our Saviour has made every provision for guarding us lest we snatch ourselves out of His hand. The victory over sin which is secured from faith in Christ is, however, a moment by moment victory, and we must ever be "looking unto Jesus, the Beginner and Finisher of our faith" (Heb. 12:2).

But thanks be to God, it isn't our "looking unto Jesus" that gives us the victory, but "His looking unto us." Peter could see the Lord despitefully used, and whilst looking at Him could curse and deny that he knew Him. But when our "Saviour turned and looked upon Peter" no further denial was possible. Not our faith, but His faithfulness is our safeguard.

The indwelling Christ is more than equal to all emergencies. So long as we trust Him fully and obey His smallest behest — so long shall we continue in victory. Why then should a man ever commit any voluntary sin? And why are we surprised when a fully sanctified Christian man tells us he never sins knowingly?

The Cause of Failure

The reason why even fully consecrated Christians are sometimes "overtaken in a fault" is because the majority of believers are not fully surrendered to the will of God. It would be safe to say that most Christians think very little of such sins as pride, anger, irritability, impatience, jealousy, self-seeking, unlove and suchlike. It is, therefore, such an easy thing for a man living the Victorious Life to fall into any of these sins; so many of his fellow-Christians do so unblushingly. And should he fall probably no one is in the least surprised at it! Moreover, no one but a wholly sanctified man can reprove such a one, or he will get the reply, "Physician, heal thyself," or even be referred to the "beam" and the "mote." In fact, only a "spiritual" man can help him. As St. Paul says, "If a man be overtaken in a fault, ye which are spiritual restore such a one" (Gal. 6:1).

Yet how easy it is to live the life of victory when in the company of wholly sanctified men and women! Oh, that there were many more such!

Why are we surprised when a man says he has reached a state of "sinless perfection"? Well, as a rule it is perfectly obvious to anyone but himself that he has not reached such an ideal. Sooner or later he is "overtaken in a fault." A saintly Christian man was recently arguing this point at a big luncheon party, and he claimed "sinless perfection" for himself. A fellow guest quietly said, whether in sincerity, or as a test, I know not, "Forgive me for saying so, but I was thinking you were a little greedy over your food!" "I've never yet been accused of greed over anything," flashed out the reply, "nor will I allow *you* to accuse me!" The warmth with which the retort was made raised a smile on the faces of all who heard it; practice and profession so evidently disagreed.

This little story proves both the statements made above. The "sinlessly perfect" man is sometimes irritable and angry, and when he is "overtaken in a fault" the average Christian is both amused and pleased!

Sins or "Infirmities"

The writer has had the privilege of meeting believers who claim "sinless perfection." He sat at a table with one at every meal for a week. To be quite frank he must acknowledge that he saw no outward trace of any sin. But this dear child of God took the writer to task in a kindly way for not preaching sinless perfection. This led to a long chat on the subject. My critic declared that a violent temper had been completely eradicated by the Lord Jesus. But he confessed to occasional feelings of impatience, irritability, and unlove. "These, however, I regard as *infirmities* and not as sins," said he.

My experience is that when men who profess sinless perfection are tackled about it they always maintain that "little" things which *we* call sins are only infirmities. Brothers, take your infirmities to Christ, and let the "strength of Christ rest upon you" (2 Cor. 12:9).

Sometimes, alas! great harm is done to the cause of Christ by men professing "sinless perfection," and boasting about it, even while allowing things in their lives which give the lie to their profession.

One such came to a friend of the writer to consult him on a business question. It was such an obvious case of sharp practice, if not of downright dishonesty, that my friend said in surprise, "How does such an act fit in with your profession of sinless perfection?" "Oh, business is business," came the impatient reply. "And I will have nothing to do with this piece of business, then," answered my friend.

We have dwelt at length on this point because the devil uses the bogey of "sinless perfection" to scare away many sincere souls from seeking a life of holiness.

Our position is just this: So long as a fully surrendered believer simply trusts the Lord Jesus to keep him and to conquer his temptations for him he need not commit willful sin. It is, therefore, quite legitimate and right and fitting that we should pray every morning, "Grant that this day we fall into no sin." "Vouchsafe, O Lord, to keep us this day without sin." And Christ is able to keep us even from stumbling (Jude 24, R.V.). And He does keep us just so long as we trust Him to do so.

Yet at any moment we may fall into sin. It is a moment by moment victory. Many who read this will gladly confess to have experienced this freedom from known sin for five minutes, for ten minutes, for an hour, and for a much longer time. But we shall all sadly confess that at times we willfully harbor a sinful thought and sometimes even commit knowingly some sinful act, falling under some sudden temptation. As we look back upon it we are confident that we need not have sinned. It was "our own most grievous fault." Moreover, we find that the majority of such slips are due to unchristian acts or words of other believers. They are more often due to the low level of spiritual life in fellow-Christians than to the opposition of the world.

Do not condemn us, but claim victory for yourself and so raise the standard around us.

Claim victory for yourself, and show us by practical demonstration what a glorious life can be lived by one who is wholly Christ's.

CHAPTER XII

THE PERILS OF THIS LIFE — SOME OF THE PERILS THAT BESET A LIFE OF HOLINESS AND HOW THEY MAY BE MET AND CONQUERED

The Victorious Life is not something which is obtained once for all — a summit reached from which nothing can dislodge us. This victory is secured from moment to moment by a moment-by-moment faith. There is constant victory for the believer so long as he trusts Christ entirely — and only so long.

The moment that simple faith is lost, that moment the victory over sin is broken. That is why our Lord seems to sum up "sin" in the one word "unbelief." "The Holy Spirit when He is come shall convict the world of sin . . . of sin, because they believe not on Me" (John 16:8). And this is why St. John says, "This is the victory that overcometh the world, even our FAITH" (1 John 5:4).

Since, then, there is no such thing as once-for-all victory, it is evident that this life is beset with perils, and we must be constantly on our guard. Or, to be strictly accurate we must ever allow "the peace of God to guard our hearts." An earnest laboring man used to insist upon quoting that verse as "A piece of God shall guard your hearts" — and his idea was right. For it is the indwelling Christ, the Son of God, Who does this for us.

The Abiding Christ

What are some of the dangers that beset a life of holiness? To be forewarned is to be forearmed. Nor need we fear to face any danger. "For in all these things we are more than conquerors through Him that loved us" (Rom. 8:37).

There is, first of all —

1. Self-effort.

In the first flush of joy at realizing the possibility of such a life of victory there is a tendency to attempt to hug our possession — to make a continuous and conscious effort to cling to it. A feeling that if we do not strenuously concentrate our thoughts upon the indwelling Christ we shall lose Him. Perhaps this comes from regarding the Victorious Life as a blessing — a possession we can forfeit or lose. Satan always tries to get us to regard it as such. It may slip from our grasp. No. It is a Person, not a "thing." It is the Lord Jesus Christ Himself, Who comes not so much for us to possess Him, but that He may possess us. He cannot slip from our grasp. He holds us. He has promised, "I will never leave thee nor forsake thee" (Heb. 13:5). That is why the writer likes to dwell upon the abiding Christ rather than the "fulness of the Spirit."

> Once it was the blessing,
> Now it is the Lord;
> Once it was the feeling,
> Now it is His Word.
> Once His gifts I wanted,
> Now the Giver own;
> Once I sought for healing,
> Now Himself alone.

He keeps us — it is not we who keep Him, and "He is able to keep." Of course, we must allow the Lord Jesus to be "the home of our thoughts." But "looking unto Jesus" in faith and love does not mean strenuous effort to retain Him — a willing guest. Our "look" of faith is not with strained eyes, but with a restful gaze.

88

In the Place of Safety

"Abide in Me," says our Lord. Just rest peacefully in Him so far as your life of victory is concerned. At every alarm, at every approach of temptation, just "hide in Him," the Rock of Ages, just as the coney takes cover in his rock of defense. "Consider the lilies of the field, how they grow" — not by self-effort, toiling or striving. They just abide in the sunshine and drink in its life. "Which of you by being anxious can add one cubit to his stature?" asks our Lord in the Sermon on the Mount. And in His mind was something more than physical stature.

It is not our faith but His faithfulness that maintains the Victorious Life. "Trust in the Lord," and then "do good; so shalt thou dwell in the land and verily thou shalt be fed" (Ps. 37:3).

We may remark in passing that even in our conflict with evil around us our trust must be entirely in Him, and not in our own power and effort. How remarkably this is brought out in our Lord's instructions to His Apostles. "Behold, I send you forth as sheep amidst wolves," says He. Now how does He proceed? "Be ye therefore armed to the teeth?" NEVER. "Be ye therefore harmless as doves" (Matt. 10:16). Why? Because *He* is our defense and our shield.

2. *No Freedom From Temptation.*

The Victorious Life is not an untempted life. Only *one* Man has ever lived an unbroken Victorious Life, and that was our Lord Himself. And "He was tempted in all points like as we are, yet without sin." The sinless angels were tempted, and some fell. Adam and Eve in their sinless state were tempted, and also fell. So let us not be surprised when the devil tempts us. He will do all in his power to drag us down, because the Victorious Life is the only one that really counts. Every child of God will be tempted, but we can "count it all joy," for we are told that the shield of faith is "able to quench ALL the fiery darts of the evil one" (Eph. 6:16).

89

A Constant Attitude of Faith

3. If We Fall.

There is always the possibility of sinning, and there is the provision for it. "If the priest that is anointed do sin as the people . . ." (Lev. 4:3). "Doesn't this prove that sin is inevitable?" asked an inquirer. Surely not. Every ship that sails is provided with a supply of lifeboats, lest there should be a shipwreck or a collision.

This does not imply that it is the captain's intention to wreck his ship; nor does it mean that therefore every ship must be wrecked.

So, then, it is possible for both priest and people to sin.

The Victorious Life is secured by an act of faith: and it is only maintained by a constant attitude of faith. Suppose, then, there is a momentary failure and we fall into some sin. What then? Why, Satan immediately tries to follow up his victory by trying to persuade us that there is no such thing as the Victorious Life; or that if there is, then we never had the blessing; or if we had — well, it is gone forever: we've lost it. And our fellow-Christians who have never seen the only way of victory will gladly back him up in his assertions. Even devout and earnest believers will assure us that such teaching is a dangerous heresy.

Do not listen either to Satan or them. We have seen that the Bible is full of Victorious Life teaching. This "dangerous heresy" was taught by Christ, and shows itself again and again in St. Paul's Epistles and those of St. John.

Remember that God gave us the Victorious Life after many, many falls. Will He then withhold it forever because of one more fall? Surely not!

Satan's Whisperings

But if Satan fails in dissuading you from again attempting to live a life of victory he will try to delay your recovery. He will whisper that after such a grievous failure you must lie low for a while; it will take a long time for you to get back again into the life of victory; there must be an arduous climb, a tedious and humbling process of recovery. What answer will you give him?

Now we have conclusively shown that no striving or struggling on our part will ever bring us victory in the first place.

It must, therefore,,be obvious that such effort and struggling will never reinstate us! If we fall into any sin, our Saviour wishes us at once to turn to Him in faith for forgiveness.

Instant forgiveness and instant restoration. Even in the Old Testament dispensation this was so. "I have sinned against the Lord," said the penitent king. "The Lord also hath put away thy sin," replied the prophet immediately.

"If we confess our sins He is faithful and just to forgive us our sins, and to cleanse us from all unrighteousness" (1 John 1:9). Your fall does not weaken Christ. "He is (still) able to keep." HE has not failed. Nor will He fail you. And once you are forgiven, turn your thoughts away from that sin and try never to think of it again. "One thing I do," said Paul, "forgetting the things [he might well have said "sins"] that are behind . . . I press on toward the goal" (Phil. 3:13).

A Hindrance to Holiness

This is not minimizing or underrating the sin. No one has such a horror of sin as he who is living the Victorious Life. Nor does it mean complacency under defeat.

But we feel strongly that the recollection of past sins is one of the greatest hindrances to present holiness and usefulness. Such recollection weakens our confidence, prevents our usefulness, and reminds us of the "pleasures of sin": so there follow feeble witness, fruitless work, and fresh falling into sin.

Moreover, remorse, or agony of feeling, or self-condemnation, cannot do aught to heal the wound. The atoning blood of Christ is sufficient for that. In fact, so sufficient — if one may use such an expression — that after the gift of the Holy Spirit at Pentecost Christians are nowhere told to pray for the forgiveness of their sins. The command is simply to confess them to God, and their forgiveness is assured.

The reason is obvious. When the Holy Spirit of Christ dwells in the heart, sin is abhorrent, and a longing for forgiveness always accompanies confession.

4. *Do Not Presume*.

"The truth about the indwelling Christ, or rather the consciousness of His indwelling, gives you such wonderful confidence," said a venerable cleric to the writer, "that the danger is that you get *too* confident." We see his point. But we cannot be too confident! What this man of God meant is this: There is a danger of relying upon past victory to keep us safe in the present. We may have — and Christ desires us to have — a long period of unbroken victory.

But the longer the period, the safer and stronger we are apt to *feel* ourselves to be. Paul knew the danger full well, "Let him that thinketh he standeth take heed lest he fall" (1 Cor. 10:12). We must bear in mind that *our* weakness is never made strong. "Our sufficiency is from God." We are NEVER sufficient of ourselves to account anything as from ourselves (2 Cor. 3:5).

It is "All of Christ" and always of Christ.

"It is God that worketh in you both to will and to do" (Phil. 2:13). As Mr. C. G. Trumbull puts it (in his *Perils of the Victorious Life*):

"Christ and Christ alone is our victory. Ten years of unbroken record does not add a particle to the strength of our Lord Jesus Christ; it does not increase the sufficiency of His grace, for that sufficiency is infinite. The assurance of our continuance in victory is not our good record, but the grace of our Lord. Our continued record in victory adds nothing to our assurance of victory."

The Necessity of Obedience

Moreover our victory for any length of time does not weaken Satan. *He* is just as powerful and active and spiteful, and just waits his opportunity. And *his* opportunity is any over-confidence or spiritual pride in us.

5. *Disobey Not Our Lord's Command.*

A radiantly happy couple wished to speak to me after an address on the indwelling Christ. "We have known and experienced the truth of the Victorious Life for many months now," said the husband, "and it has completely revolutionized our lives. All this time we have been staying away from the Lord's Table. We never go to the Holy Communion now. But are we right in keeping away?" "What is your *reason* for absenting yourselves?" I asked. "Because Paul tells us there is no further need of the Holy Communion when once Christ has come to dwell in the heart," was the astonishing reply. With much curiosity the writer asked for the reference to such a command. And this was the answer: "Paul said, 'As oft as ye eat this bread and drink this cup ye proclaim the Lord's death *till He come*' (1 Cor. 11:26). Well, now that He *has* come to abide *in* us, we have refrained from partaking of the Holy Communion." That godly man and woman were delighted to learn that those words "Till He come" evidently refer to the Second Coming of our Lord. Paul himself was then living and preaching the Victorious Life, but he still partook of the Holy Communion. "We *all* partake of the one bread," says he (1 Cor. 10:17). We must never disobey any command of our Lord.

Yet how gracious our Lord is! The dear people mentioned above were radiantly happy and were bringing forth "the fruit of the Spirit," although they were disobeying God. They "did it ignorantly," but not in unbelief, and the Saviour graciously blessed them and in due time showed them the "better way."

Indwelt by the Holy Trinity

The writer has met advanced Churchmen of the Anglo-Catholic school — holy and humble men of God — who have been thrilled by talks on the Victorious Life, but who have expressed a fear that such teaching would "do away with the need of the Sacrament.'' No such fear need ever disturb their minds.

This teaching is entirely Scriptural, as we have shown.

Space forbids us to enter fully into the relationship between the indwelling of Christ through the Holy Spirit and our Lord's definite declaration, ''Except ye eat the flesh of the Son of Man and drink His blood ye have not life in yourselves'' (John 6:53).

Let us remind ourselves that all the Persons of the Trinity dwell in us. Christ said, ''If a man love Me he will keep My word: and My Father will love him, and WE will come unto him, and make our abode with him'' (John 14:23). We know that the Holy Spirit dwelleth in us ''that He may abide with you for ever'' (14:16).

It may be that God the Father, God the Son, and God the Holy Spirit ''sanctify us wholly'' — soul, body and spirit.

But we do believe that no victory ever admits of disobedience to any of our Lord's commands. And when He says, ''Do this,'' we must obey. If we love Him we shall keep His commandments.

Chapter XIII

OTHER PERILS

*Some More of the Perils That Beset the Path of the
True Seeker After Holiness*

There are other perils in the path of holiness in addition
to those already dealt with. Let us look at them.

Where Many Blunder

6. *Do Not Assume Infallibility.*

We can picture many of our readers smiling at such a
ridiculous counsel. But this is a real danger! There is such
a joy in unbroken communion with our Lord, and often such
a consciousness of power — not our power, but that of the
indwelling Christ — that there is a danger of our supposing
that we always know God's will in any matter — that we are
always right.

The writer once had occasion to live with four consecrated men of God — all of them far more experienced in
holy living than himself. One of them was, indeed, deeply
taught of God and used to spend long hours in prayer. But in
our deliberations he always quietly assumed that he had the
mind of Christ, and that any proposal which conflicted with

his ideas must necessarily be wrong; and this, even if four of us felt led another way to that suggested by him. Not infrequently, subsequent events showed that we were right and he was wrong.

One morning our leader quietly and kindly remarked, "My dear——, some of us think that we also are led to God." Do not misunderstand me. The reference here is not to a obstinate, dogmatic, self-opinioned man who wished to have his own way. Our friend in question was holy, humble, and unselfish to a degree — but was "infallible." He always assumed that he was absolutely guided by God in all his proposals. The best of us is not a little deaf spiritually, and we do not always catch God's message; just as a deaf person does not always catch the right message through a telephone. There must be a perfect "doing of God's will" before there is a perfect "knowing of the doctrine" (John 7:17).

Let us recognize that we are fallible. We may be mistaken. This does not mean that the majority is always right. Ten men once said, "We are not able to go up against the people for they are stronger than we." Whilst only two men urged, "Let us go up at once and possess it: for we are well able to overcome it" (Num. 13:30). The people sided with the ten and years of misery and rebellion ensued, because the two were right and had the mind of God.

The World and Its Claims

7. *Do Not Ignore This World.*

A consecrated man of God lives in a house called "Torthorwold." His neighbors say that is what he lives for — "T'other world." But all who know him are aware that he leads a most strenuous life trying to make this world and its inhabitants better. We live in two worlds at the same time and have a duty to each.

"Do you think it is wrong of me to play marbles with my little boy of four?" asked a white-haired saintly father. We wonder what answer our readers would give?

How it would delight the heart of Satan if he could

persuade all wholly sanctified people that all pleasures were sinful! Dear man of God, by all means play marbles — if you are not tempted to cheat!

We are living not only a spiritual life, but a bodily life, and whether we like it or not, a very large part of our time and interests is taken up with things which concern the body. Moreover, we are placed in communities. God never meant man to live alone. God made two statements about the first man, Adam, right at the beginning of his existence.

The first was that he was "very good." The next remark was this, "it is not good that the man should be alone" (Gen. 2:18). Every man is born into a family — every man has his human relationships. Each of us is to show love to all men. All the little social amenities of life are points of contact with those around us. Love manifests itself in deeds, and we must be human as well as "divine." We can only show our love to God by deeds of love to our fellow-men. By all means romp with the little ones and play with the big ones!

Happy and "Human"

Men living the Victorious Life are the happiest and "humanest" of people, overflowing with the joy of the Lord — bubbling over with innocent fun and mirth. We are here to make this world a happier world. "The joy of the Lord is your strength" (Neh. 8:10). We are to "rejoice evermore," and that means we are to begin now, here on earth.

A mother sat searching her Bible, trying to probe the secrets of a life of holiness. She spent so much time seeking spiritual help that the duties of her household became irksome and were either hurried through or neglected. The "homeliness" of home was gone. One day, as she was deep in study, her little girl toddled up to her side with a broken doll. "Mummy, please mend dolly for me." With an impatient gesture, the mother brushed the little one aside. "I've more important things to do than trouble about dolly!" The little one turned sadly away, and the mother continued her search for holiness.

But the search was a fruitless one, and the mother closed

her book with a sigh, and sought the little child. She was lying on the hearthrug clutching her darling doll, and with the tears still wet on her pretty face. The mother's heart was smitten. God spoke to her then and there. Tenderly stooping over the little one she woke her with her kisses. Then taking her into her arms she breathed a prayer to God for forgiveness. She saw that holiness could not thrive on neglected duties. Her devotion to her Lord was henceforth seen in her care of the household, and shone out even in mending broken toys! Home became home again. And the very page of Scripture was lighted up with a fresh glory.

Yes, and victory shone in the mother's radiant face.

The Christian Heritage

We believe that the Lord Jesus, Who watched the children at their play, and the fishermen and farmers at their work, Who worked Himself and yet made time to be present at a wedding feast, wishes us to take a real and lively interest in all the concerns of life — our own and those of our friends. He has given us a capacity for pleasure, and He longs to see us enjoy His gift of life.

He has given us a physical frame which needs food, and work, exercise, and relaxation. He wishes us to enjoy our meals, our work, and our recreation. The marvelous realm of nature, the wonderful infinitude of space peopled with suns, the cadence of music and the color of sky and sea and landscape are for our enjoyment.

> All things bright and beautiful,
>   All creatures great and small,
> All things wise and wonderful,
>   The Lord God made them all

for our pleasure as well as for His glory.

> The world is so full of a number of things
> I'm sure we should all be as happy as kings,

says the child's poet. God expects His children to be careful about their dress and manners. Surely He desires us to be attractive Christians? The King's business requires haste, but

98

it never requires discourtesy or lack of proper attentiveness to our fellows.

Is Religion Misery?

The writer met a godly major on a voyage to India. He had been converted from a life of dissolution and was now ever engrossed in his Bible. He avoided every kind of amusement — even deck quoits. Writing to me from a public school in England a son of the dear major said, "I *am* so glad you have met my father. Do try to convert him to the Church of England; his religion makes him so miserable."

No wonder the high-spirited lad found little happiness in his father's company, and was a little shy of "religion."

God's religion never yet made a man miserable! Nor does the Lord Jesus delight in misery! Did not the Saviour say, "These things have I spoken unto you that My joy might remain in you, and that your joy might be full" (John 15:11)? There is a *right* way of "making the most of both worlds."

Not Trusting to Thrills

8. *Do Not Rely on Thrills*.

If often happens that when a believer enters upon a life of victory over voluntary sin that he experiences a joy, and an ecstasy and a thrill which make him feel as if he were treading on air. But this is not always the case, and we must not suppose that an absence of thrills is a proof that Christ has not come in His fullness.

God wants us to trust Him and His Word, and not to rely upon feelings. He would save us from the peril of testing our victory, or testing His indwelling, by any preconceived notions of ours as to *how* His presence shall be felt or manifested. Think less of the victory, less of the blessing, and more of the Blesser.

You remember Spurgeon's apt remark, which is worth repeating just here. "I looked at Jesus and the dove of peace flew into my heart. I looked at the dove of peace and she flew away."

Do not then be examining or testing your victory. Maintain a simple and constant trust in Christ — *He* cannot fail.

It is really better to enter into the Victorious Life by simple faith unaccompanied by ecstasy or thrill.

For when the thrill subsides, and life seems humdrum and commonplace, we may be tempted to think that the victory has vanished with the thrill! Fact — faith — feeling: that is the order.

9. *Do Not be Surprised if Others Fail to See Our Victory.*

Only One Man ever lived a sinless life — a really Victorious Life all through — and that is the Man Christ Jesus.

But the leaders of religion in His days on earth were so blinded that they failed to see the Victorious Life in Him. They called Him a "wine-bibber."

"We know that this man is a sinner," said they of Christ. So we must not be surprised if men fail to recognize the Victorious Life in us.

We must be very humble, and when others thwart us or oppose us, and deny our sincerity or orthodoxy, no spirit of unlove or root of bitterness must come in; no holier-than-thou feeling must be entertained for a moment — or our victory is broken.

We are certain to be misunderstood, and our greatest opponents will be not the world, but the Church!

The devil has sown tares in the field of the Church, and only God Himself knows what is tares and what is wheat. It is from these — the children of the wicked one in the Church — that the greatest opposition is to be expected. [Our Lord never calls mere unbelievers "children of the devil," but only "religious" unbelievers (see Matt. 13:25,38; 23:15; John 8:38-44). It is an awful thought, but must be noted.] The servant is not greater than his Lord. If Christ received opposition from "religious" people, so shall we.

But every such act of opposition is an opportunity for us to show, not by our lip, but by our life, the Christ-life; to prove that there *is* victory through the Lord Jesus Christ.

And even if some oppose and criticize and condemn, many around us, seeing our victory through Christ, will be glad thereof and rejoice; because they will see the mighty power of God — mighty to the overthrowing of strongholds.

The Moment of Victory

10. *Now — Not Tomorrow.*

May we remind our readers of a very simple fact, and yet one so often forgotten. It is this: The only time you can live the Victorious Life is Now.

The only way to have Victory through Christ is to get it Now — at this very moment. This life is not merely one for emergencies. So many dear people are waiting for future opportunities to manifest the indwelling Christ.

They wait for a prayer meeting, or an open-air, or for a conversation with another congenial spirit.

But Now is the only moment of victory.

God is Light as well as Love. And our Lord said, "*Let* your light shine" — not *make* it shine as occasion arises. LET IT shine always, everywhere.

When you spring out of bed each day and say joyously to yourself and your God, "To me to live is Christ," make up your mind to manifest something of the glory of Christ to everyone you meet that day. Keep a watch over yourself.

Let the people in the home see the light — the victory. Let your fellow-workers in the office or yard, in the shop or the ship, the factory or the school, see that Christ is dwelling in your heart. Why should not the tradesman, the postmen, the bus-conductors detect your secret? Be epistles of Christ, "known and read of all men" (2 Cor. 3:2).

A dear friend of the writer's — a cultured man brought literally to the gutter through drink — was converted at a tramps' mission. The day following, he boarded a tram. The conductor was mystified, for the passenger's clothes told of beggary, whilst his face reflected heaven! "Why, mate," he exclaimed, "you look as if someone's died and left you a fortune!" "You are right there," came the quick reply.

"Jesus Christ has died for me and has given me His riches in glory." "Well, he might dress you better," was the sneer — and He Did.

Shall not even strangers be attracted by our joy?

In Communion With Christ

But do not wait for the future. Let victory be yours Now.

Just live in such communion with Christ that He can always show forth His glory through you.

"Unto me was this grace given, to preach unto the Gentiles the unsearchable riches of Christ, to make All Men see what is the mystery which from all ages hath been hid in God . . . that Now might be made known through the Church [*i.e.,* through you and me] the manifold wisdom of God" (Eph. 3:9,10).

Yes — and His wondrous life and ineffable glory.

Chapter XIV

"HIGHEST" CRITICISM

*The Highest Criticism That Prevents Many
Christians From Believing and Accepting
Their Rich Heritage in Christ*

The most extraordinary thing about the Victorious Life is that although it is so clearly taught in Scripture, yet it is so frequently unrecognized by Bible students. Many who have a thorough knowledge of their Bibles know nothing of this truth experientially. The writer himself had been a careful student of the Scriptures for many years before the glory of this life lighted up his soul. Again and again clergy have confessed, "We do not preach this truth because we do not know it experientially."

How is it that we are so slow of heart to understand? Probably the best way to put the case is to describe at some length the inner experiences of two men who had been devoted to the service of God. Hudson Taylor, then a missionary in China, was one of these men. He has left in a letter to his sister a record of his search for holiness and his total inability to see how to get it, although the way lies so clearly on the page of Scripture. This is his confession:

Hudson Taylor's Confession

"I prayed, fasted, agonized, strove, made resolutions, read the Bible more diligently, sought more time for retirement and meditation — but all without effect. Every day — almost every hour — the consciousness of sin oppressed me. Then came the question: 'Is there no rescue? Must it be this to the end — constant conflict, and instead of Victory, too often defeat?' I hated myself, I hated my sin, and yet I gained no strength against it. I felt I was a child of God, but how to rise to my privileges as a child I was utterly powerless to see. I thought that holiness, practical holiness, was to be gradually attained by a diligent use of the means of grace. I felt there was nothing I so much desired in the world, nothing I so much needed. When my agony of soul was at its height a sentence in a letter was used to remove the scales from my eyes, and the Spirit of God revealed the truth of our oneness with Jesus."

What was this letter? What was the sentence? The letter runs: "By faith a channel is formed by which Christ's fulness plenteously flows down. The barren branch becomes a portion of the fruitful stem. He is most holy who has most of Christ within. It is defective faith which clogs the feet and causes many a fall. Abiding — not struggling or striving: looking off to Him; trusting Him for present power; trusting Him to subdue all inward corruption; resting in the conscious joy of a complete salvation; a salvation from all sin: willing that He should be truly supreme. That is NOT NEW, YET IT IS NEW TO ME. I seem to have got to the edge only, but to the edge of a sea that is boundless. Christ literally ALL seems to me now the power, the only power for service; the only ground for unchanging joy. Now, then, is this faith increased? Only by thinking of all that JESUS is and all that He is for us: His life, His death, His work, HIMSELF, as revealed to us in His Word, to be the subject of our constant thoughts. *Not a striving to have faith,* or to increase our faith, *but a looking off to the* FAITHFUL ONE seems all we need — a resting in the Loved One entirely for time and eternity. It

DOES NOT APPEAR TO ME ANYTHING NEW — only formerly misapprehended."

From Failure to Triumph

That was the letter, and the sentence which arrested Hudson Taylor's attention was the last one — "Not a striving to have faith, but a looking off to the Faithful One seems all we need."

We have quoted these letters at length, partly because they sum up all we have been trying to teach in these pages; but chiefly because both these men of God confess that such teaching is NOT NEW, yet both have failed to apprehend it, although they were simply yearning for a life of Victory.

As the writer looks back on his past life, nothing so surprises him as the fact that he failed to see, or grasp, or apprehend this Victorious Life teaching, although it is not new, although it is so plainly taught in Scripture.

Why is this? Why do so many devout scholars fail to claim, or even seek, a life of Victory? We cannot help feeling that it is because many read the Bible critically — yes, and devoutly and reverently — but without really claiming the illumination of the Holy Spirit. Many scholars will indignantly deny this. But we feel that it is so. We do not accuse anyone of deliberately rejecting the help of the Holy Spirit — but of deceiving themselves, or at least of being deceived.

Even the saintly Bishop Moule confessed that although he was Principal of a Theological College, he not only failed to grasp the meaning of this teaching, but was confident that it was wrong — unscriptural — until the light dawned. Many of our readers will remember how Bishop Moule came to see these truths when on a visit to Scotland. And all the world knows how full of it his books are.

Under the Spirit's Power

The writer would like to suggest the following as an explanation of some of our blindness. Paul says, "The letter killeth: it is the Spirit that giveth life" (2 Cor. 3:6). Unless then the Holy Spirit illuminates the Word, it is not life-giving and no Victorious Life can result. Our Lord once said, "Man shall not live by bread alone, but by every word that proceedeth out of the mouth of God" (Matt. 4:4). Not by every word that proceeded. The word is in the present tense, "proceedeth." Now the word is always proceeding. That is to say, the Holy Spirit takes the "letter that killeth" and brings it home with power and life to the hearts of those who rely upon Him to do so.

The disciples had heard many things they could not understand — hard sayings — but Christ said, "When He, the Spirit of truth is come, He shall guide you into all the truth; for He shall not speak from Himself, but what things soever He shall bear, these shall He speak" (John 16:13). Now we live by the same written word which the Lord *is speaking* to us through the Holy Spirit — the word which, through the Spirit, is still "proceeding" out of the mouth of God.

The Holy Spirit is called in the Nicene Creed "The Lord and Giver of Life." It is He Who gives us the Victorious Life. But He does it by revealing to us the WORD OF GOD — not only the meaning of the written word, but by giving us the indwelling Christ — The "WORD." Christ is born in us, as it were, and lives in us "by the operation of the Holy Ghost."

One is often asked the question: "Is the Victorious Life the same thing as the fullness of the Holy Spirit?" Well, what is the work of the Holy Spirit? He comes in all His fullness not to speak for Himself, but to reveal the Lord Jesus Christ, and to lead us into all truth. "He shall glorify Me," says Christ, "for He shall take of Mine and shall declare it unto you."

Where So Many Fail

"There is nothing new in all this!" is the impatient, well-nigh querulous comment so often made concerning this teaching. But the very tone of voice betrays an unwillingness to attempt to really assimilate this ancient teaching.

The real trouble is that so many people who deplore higher criticism, themselves indulge in what we venture to call Highest criticism. They must acknowledge that this Victorious Life is scriptural, but they openly declare that it is impossible. They do not deny the truth of the Word of God, but they tacitly believe that it is unworkable. Oh, if we could only just take Christ at His word! If we only had a simple childlike faith in God!

> If our faith were but more simple
> We should take Him at His word;
> And our lives would be all sunshine
> In the glory of the Lord.

Let us explain what we mean by highest criticism. We mean absolutely refusing to believe that it is possible to obey all God's commands. Now the joy which is inseparable from the Victorious Life is from just taking God at His word.

Take such a definite command as Philippians 4:6, "In nothing be anxious." Do we obey it? Do we believe it is God's will that we should never have an anxious thought? Many Christian people must sadly confess that their experience is that they are anxious about everything. The writer consulted an eminent physician, a few years back, who expressed an opinion — wrongly, as events proved — that the heart was overstrained and that a long rest was imperative. Anxiety was clearly noted by the doctor, for he said, "May I make a remark about you clergy? Many people consult me, but I find that you leaders of religion are *just as anxious* about your bodies as men who profess no religion at all." What a rebuke! The writer stood condemned — and felt condemned; but his anxiety still remained! Why? Simply because he did not know the secret of the indwelling Christ.

Sure of Three Things

He was not acting up to what he professed to believe. He had often quoted to others the God-given command, "Cast thy burden upon the Lord and He shall sustain THEE" (Ps. 55:22). "Casting ALL YOUR ANXIETY upon Him, for He careth for you" (1 Peter 5:7). Yet here he was, anxious and troubled over his physical condition, when God's very plain and definite command is "In nothing be anxious."

There was clearly something wrong with the spiritual life. What was it? Not blind unbelief, but blank unbelief!

"We may be quite sure of three things," says Francis Ridley Havergal. "First, that whatever our Lord commands us, He really means us to do.

"Secondly, that whatever He commands us is 'for our good always.'

"And thirdly, that whatever He commands He is able and willing to enable us to do, for 'all God's biddings are enablings.' "

Now is there any reason for the slightest anxiety in one wholly surrendered to God? Dare we ever doubt His love or His ability to provide for us? Why, if a believer only obeys this one command of God, "In nothing be anxious," he finds heaven begun on earth below. But it is impossible for *me* to keep that command.

So Christ just comes to dwell in my heart, to live His life in me, and to do what I myself cannot do.

> Said the sparrow to the robin:
> "I should really like to know
> Why these anxious human beings
> Rush about and worry so."
> Said the robin to the sparrow:
> "Friend, I think that it must be
> That they have no Heavenly Father
> Such as cares for you and me."

Now we *do* know our Heavenly Father, Who gave us His own Son. "Shall He not also with Him freely give us all things?" (Rom. 8:32). Then why be anxious?

If you really desire the Victorious Life you must "Cast — 'roll off' the word means — all your anxiety upon Him." For if you keep any of your worry, there is something wrong with your spiritual life and you cannot enjoy the life more abundant; for you fail to trust God.

Now Christ, living in you, can alone give you miraculous power to obey His command, "In nothing be anxious."

Do We Believe God's Word?

We were speaking a little time back about the possibility of freedom from sinning. There are two very definite statements in Scripture which show that Christians need not commit known sins. One is in Ephesians 6:16, "Taking the shield of faith, wherewith ye shall be able to quench all the fiery darts of the evil one." The other is this: "God is faithful, Who will not suffer you to be tempted above that we are able; but will with the temptation make also the way of escape, that ye may be able to endure it" (1 Cor. 10:13).

These are really very wonderful statements. What a glorious possibility is here held out to us! For this includes the great root sin of unbelief. Every sorrow comes through sin — every worry comes through sin. And there is a possible Victory over every sin through Jesus Christ our Lord.

The question is, do we believe God's Word or do we not? The usual up-and-down experience of the Christian is not God's plan for him. If we really believe that the indwelling Christ can do this thing for us, then let us trust Him to do it.

There is another comforting *fact* given in the Bible. God says, "My grace is sufficient for thee" (2 Cor. 12:9). This is not a promise; it is a FACT — an unchangeable, unmoving fact. The writer made this remark at a meeting, and a lady came up to him immediately afterwards and said, "But you left out the condition." "What condition?" "Why, there must be faith before God's grace can be sufficient," said she. But, dear reader, whether you have faith or whether you have not, does not and cannot alter a FACT! "God's grace is sufficient for you," whether you believe it or not. There was always "bread enough and to spare" in the Father's house, even when the prodigal was in a far country desiring to be fed upon the husks the swine did eat! Always enough and to spare — He had only to go and share it.

God's grace is always sufficient. God Himself has declared it to be so. When sudden temptation comes upon you unawares, do you stop to pray for deliverance from it — or do you look to Christ for victory over it? Someone has said, "When tempted, do not begin to ask *how* can I get out of it, but *what* can I get out of it?" "The peace of God, which passeth all understanding, shall guard your hearts and YOUR THOUGHTS in Christ Jesus" (Phil. 4:7 R.V.). The Lord Jesus is dwelling in the heart to banish even the thought of evil before it can become sin.

If you are troubled with evil thoughts, claim this promise — that the indwelling Christ can indeed guard our "thoughts."

It was this verse, "My grace is sufficient for thee," which led that veteran Christian warrior, Preb. Webb-Peploe, into the Victorious Life. After the crushing sorrow of losing a beloved child he tried to prepare a sermon with this as his text. But he could not "cast his burden upon the Lord." Rising to his feet he cried out to God in his agony, "Oh, God, it is not true. I do not find Thy Grace sufficient for me in this heavy sorrow that has befallen me. But, oh, *make* it sufficient."

A Great Experience

Falling on his knees he repeated this prayer. Then through his tears he saw over the mantelpiece an illuminated plaque, "My grace is sufficient." In a flash he saw his mistake! "What a fool I am," he cried. "How dare I ask God to *make* what is! I will get up and trust Him." And he did trust Him. We all know what the entrance into the Victorious Life meant for Webb-Peploe, and, through him, for the whole world! So also Paul, who knew that God's grace was sufficient, could promise this: "My God shall fulfill every need of yours according to His RICHES IN GLORY (what a treasury!) IN CHRIST JESUS (what a Saviour!)" (Phil. 4:19).

Fellow-Christian, can you conceive any greater promise?

This supply is moment by moment. The manna just fell day by day. As one dear saint has said, "God gave me a great fortune — placed thousands and millions to my credit. But gave me a checkbook, with this one condition, 'You never can draw more than you need at the time.' "

We have to learn to take from Him our spiritual life every second.

Just one other command — as binding as "thou shalt not steal." It is this. "Rejoice in the Lord." Have you thought out what these words mean? It is not a call to rejoice in our oneness with Him; or in the means of grace given us; or His work in us; or in our fellowship with Him. We are not bidden so much to rejoice in what He is to us, or what He is working in us, but just to rejoice in HIM — in HIM HIMSELF — to rejoice in what He is and has in Himself.

Do you not see what a wonderful cause of rejoicing this is? If our joy consists in His giving us victory over sin, our joy goes if we are overtaken in a fault. If our joy rests upon His work in and through us, we may not always be conscious of just what He is accomplishing, and we may be exalted or cast down unduly.

But if our joy is in HIM and what HE IS, that cannot change or fluctuate, and we can always abound in joy. Rejoice in the Lord: "Jesus Christ, Whom having not seen ye love; in Whom, though now ye see Him not, yet believing, ye rejoice greatly with joy unspeakable and full of glory" (1 Peter 1:8); "He that glorieth let him glory in the Lord" (1 Cor. 1:31); "O magnify the LORD with me!" Think often of Him. Let His wondrous glory be the theme of your thoughts and your songs. Ever recollect that it is HE — This glorious One — Who dwells in your heart by faith. And if He is supreme then you can say, "I live, yet not I, but Christ liveth in me," and joyfully add, TO ME TO LIVE IS CHRIST.

CHAPTER XV

DAYS OF HEAVEN ON EARTH

*From the Gloom and Disappointment of the
Wilderness Experience to the Glory and
Abundance of the Promised Land*

There is only one thing now to be considered, and that is
the sort of life God expects His children to live.

For Our Admonition

Before we look at that ideal — a POSSIBLE ideal — we
must just give a glance at the wonderful object lesson given
us in the redemption of God's people, Israel. Paul tells us that
the experiences of the children of Israel, in their deliverance
from Egypt and their journey to the Promised Land, are
"ensamples," or types, and that they are written for our
admonition (1 Cor. 10:11). They are full of instruction. God
means us to study the failures and failings of His chosen
people, and to take warning lest we also suffer for having an
evil heart of unbelief.

Egypt is a type of the world — Sin. Canaan, the land of
promise, is a type of Sanctification — the Victorious Life
here below.

No Egyptian taskmaster was ever more merciless and cruel than sin is. The Israelites could not save themselves. The more they struggled to get free, the harder their burdens became. So likewise the sinner cannot save himself. His struggles and efforts avail nothing. Salvation is all of grace.

Then came God's deliverance through the shedding of blood. That passover lamb was a type of Christ. "Christ our Passover is sacrificed for us" (1 Cor. 5:7). The lamb was slain and the blood shed. That was substitution. "That lamb dies instead of me," a Jew might have truly said.

Yet that blood *shed* saved no one. To effect salvation, it must be sprinkled upon the door-posts and upon the lintel. That is to say, there must be an individual claiming and acceptance of that substitutionary sacrifice. Only the blood *sprinkled* saved anyone. "Christ died for the ungodly." But if I am not to die for my sins, I must accept Christ's death in my stead. "As many as received Him, to them gave He the right to become the sons of God" (John 1:12).

THE RED SEA. — Then came that miraculous passage through the Red Sea, which Paul likens unto baptism. "Our fathers were baptized into Moses in the cloud and in the sea" (1 Cor. 10:2), although neither the waters of the sea nor the cloud touched them, and not until the passage of the Jordan did they become fully sanctified.

What did the Red Sea accomplish for the Israelites? Before they crossed it they were redeemed by the shed blood appropriated, but were still living and moving amongst their foes.

Two Aspects of Christ's Death

They were subjected to a merciless pursuit and a determined attempt to drag them back into bondage. When once they had passed through the sea, however, they were delivered from all dominion, all control of their foes. They never again had trouble from them or conflict with them. Their oppressors lay DEAD on the seashore.

What does this mean for us? Remember that there are two aspects of Christ's death. He died for our sins. He died for us—substitution. But then Paul tells us that we are also to die with Him. "I have been crucified WITH CHRIST" (Gal. 2:20); "Reckon ye yourselves to be dead indeed unto sin" (Rom. 6:11). The Israelites in bondage were delivered by the blood shed and sprinkled. But they are pursued by certain of their foes. These foes are slain at the Red Sea, but they themselves escape and are free. Egypt stands for the world of sin. Christ found us in "Egypt," and by His death in our stead delivered us from the penalty of sin. But even after our conversion some of these sins followed us and harassed us— temper, pride, jealousy, lust, worry, avarice — causing discomfiture and misery, and occasionally temporary defeat. Where is there any escape, any real victory? Only through the Red Sea — baptism, or what baptism implies; *i.e.,* a death to sin and a rising again to righteousness. That is a crucifixion with Christ, so as to be able to "reckon ourselves dead indeed unto sin."

Where Many Christians Fail

The Egyptians were seen DEAD upon the seashore. An Israelite might have gone back and have recognized his old taskmaster lying there. "There he is *dead:* he will never trouble me any more." Another might have said, "Yes, and there is my taskmaster; no more will he oppress me!"

Now it is just as true that when we enter into death with Christ we are dead to sin. We can, indeed, reckon ourselves "dead indeed unto sin" (Rom. 6:11) — to temper, pride, jealousy, avarice, lust. Hitherto such sins have been our taskmasters.

But notice that Paul does not say, "Sin is dead unto you." Those pursuing Egyptians were slain, but Egypt — sin — as a nation was still in evidence. "My personal sins I may count as 'slain' but SIN back of them all is very much alive," says one.

The reason why many Christians are constantly falling into sin is because they try to obey only one-half of Paul's injunctions. "Neither yield ye your members as instruments of unrighteousness unto sin," says St. Paul. Many attempt to act up to that. But he also says, "but yield yourselves unto God, as those alive from the dead" (Rom. 6:13). That was what Christ's death meant to our Lord Himself. He submitted His will absolutely unto God. "Lo, I come to do Thy will" (Heb. 10:9); "I do always those things that please Him," said our Lord (John 8:29). When, and so long as there is the unconditional surrender of my life to God, then "sin has NO dominion over me" (Rom. 6:14).

Deliverance From Sin

The Pass-over means deliverance from the PENALTY of SIN.

The Pass-through (the Red Sea) means deliverance from the POWER of sin.

But even in the wilderness those children of God needed to learn that in God and in Him alone they had ALWAYS ALL sufficiency in ALL things (2 Cor. 9:8).

Bitter Waters

After the children of Israel were delivered from both the bondage and power of the Egyptians, they arrive — thirsty and weary — at Marah, the bitter waters. These are at once made sweet by the WOOD thrown in. So it is still: the *wood* — the cross — that is, the *Christ* of the cross — takes the bitterness out of everything that would be otherwise galling.

But these pilgrims go on from strength to strength. From the bitter waters of Marah — that need to be sweetened — they pass on to the sweet and plenteous waters of Elim, and then on to that miraculous water which flowed out of the Rock — and "that rock was Christ" (1 Cor. 10:4); and that water a type of the Blessed Spirit.

Manna

And food was provided as well as drink. Manna — bread from heaven. Again we are taken to the cross. For Christ is our Bread from heaven — His Body broken on the cross is indeed the "bread of God . . . which cometh down from heaven and giveth life unto the world" (John 6:33).

So those pilgrims were led and fed entirely by God. The water — a type of the Holy Spirit — did not *give* life; it only sustained it. The Manna — a type of the "Bread of life" — did not *give* life, it only maintained it. The Holy Spirit, however, is "the Lord and *giver* of life." Jesus Christ is the Bread of Life — Who GIVES life, as well as sustains it.

Yet with all their manifold privileges and blessings the children of Israel "provoked God in the wilderness." Think of it! They were miraculously delivered; miraculously led; miraculously fed; miraculously preserved from sickness — for "there was not one feeble person amongst their tribes" (Ps. 105:37). Yet there were murmurings and disobedience. Their lives were not full of joy and victory.

At the Crisis of Life

But THAT was God's ideal for them — an ideal only possible *in the Promised Land*.

The Crisis of Life

So they came to Kadesh-Barnea — and there lay the land of promise before them; typical of the Victorious Life which we have outlined before the eyes of our readers.

As we read the story we expect to learn they rushed forward with joy in their hearts and songs on their lips — vying with each other as to who should be the first to enter in. Moses called the people together. "Ye are come to the mountain which the Lord our God doth GIVE unto us. Behold the Lord thy God hath set the land before thee: go up and possess it, as the Lord God of thy fathers hath said unto thee; fear not, neither be discouraged" (Deut. 1:20,21). Then the amazing thing happened: the people refused to go! "Let us first send men before us and they shall search out the land!" said they.

And Moses assented. Those people COULD NOT TRUST GOD. We all know the result. The spies return with a wonderful story and wonderful fruit. Two of their number — the two surely who carried that bunch of grapes? — said, "Let us go up AT ONCE and possess it, for we are well able to overcome it.'' But the other ten cried, ''We are not able to go up against the people, for they are stronger than we'' (Num. 13:31). Again the faithful two spoke up. ''If the Lord delight in us then HE will bring us into the land and GIVE IT TO us. Only rebel not ye against the Lord, neither fear ye the people of the land; for they are bread for us: their defence is departed from them; and the Lord is with us: fear them not.''

The Wilderness Wanderings

But the people sided with the ten and refused to obey the living God: refused to enter the land to which GOD had led them, and which GOD had promised to GIVE them. And God never gave them another chance. Not one of those people over twenty years of age, except Joshua and Caleb, ever saw the land again.

Now what does it all mean? For them it was a time of crisis. Behind them was Egypt, that gave them garlic, and leeks, and onions — and bondage. Before them was the promised land with milk and honey and luscious fruits — and FREEDOM. Which shall they choose? Thank God, they did not go back to Egypt (sin)! But, alas! they refused to enter the land of promise, where there was rest and communion with God. So they wandered for forty years in the wilderness, amid snares and noisome pestilences, and the destruction that wasteth at noonday.

What is there of ''ensample'' in all this? The Promised Land is the Victorious Life. We have tried in these articles to lead our readers right up to its borders, and we have ''looked in.'' Have we entered in? This is God's will for everyone who is trusting Him as Saviour. He wishes us to enter now, and to abide there forever. The difficulties of such a life, free from known sin, seem gigantic and insuperable. They are like the people occupying Canaan, ''Nations greater and mightier than thyself'' (Deut. 9:1).

We believe that God's command to us is, ''Go up and possess it: fear not, neither be discouraged'' (Deut. 1:21). Many believers declare the Victorious Life to be impossible: to be beyond them. ''We are unable to enter in,'' they cry.

Now God calls us to live this life in His STRENGTH, and not in our own. "If the Lord delight in us then will He bring us into the land." It means an absolute surrender of all we have and are, and a simple faith in Christ's ability to do all He has promised. Our Lord bids us go in and possess it. For, remember that "God's omnipotence is at our disposal for *keeping* as well as for service."

What the Experience Meant

The life of most Christians is simply a wilderness experience which is far removed from the rest and joy of the Promised Land.

The wilderness experience means:

1. *Restlessness*.

No settled home — no abiding-place — no possessions. At any moment they had to move on, should the cloud lift from off the tabernacle. It means discontent and murmuring against God and His providential dealings with us; murmurings against the leaders whom God has chosen; murmurings against our lot which WE have chosen (for the wilderness wanderings are really rebellion against God, and contrary to His wishes). It means, sometimes, a longing to be back in Egypt — a life of sin; and sometimes a going back.

2. *It Means Fruitlessness*.

The children of Israel fought in the wilderness but they gained nothing by their fighting except the right to go on their way unhindered. They gained no possessions. That is the ordinary life of every Christian who has not claimed the Victorious Life. It is a life made up of "not doing things." He does not dance, or play cards, or attend theaters; he, perhaps, does not even drink or smoke. But his Christian life consists of not doing wrongful or harmful things. The *fruit* of the Promised Land — the fruit of the Spirit — is not there — love, joy, peace. There is no growth in grace, and little — if any — "fruit" in service. What *seeming* results there are do not last. In the main, it is only of the one living the Victorious

Life in whom Christ's desire is fulfilled — that His "fruit should abide" (John 15:16). Many Christians have renounced the pleasures of sin — but not sin itself. They have not entered the Promised Land where true joy is found. This alone is lamentable. But the saddest part of their failure is this:

They Keep Others Out

Joshua and Caleb had a right to enter in. So had Moses. Yet the two were shut out for forty years because of the unwillingness of others to enter in! And Moses soon forfeited the right to enter in at all!

Oh, that Joshua and Caleb had refused to go with the majority! Had they but boldly marched in — they two only — we believe that God would have honored their faith, and have conquered their foes before them. Yes, and thousands would have followed in their steps. GOD CAN DO SUCH THINGS.

Jonathan and his armor-bearer knew that (1 Sam. 14:6). Moreover God offered to do it for Moses alone. "Let me alone, that I may destroy them . . . ; and I will make of THEE a nation mightier and greater than they" (Deut. 9:14).

Four Things to Remember

We have put before YOU the land of promise — the Victorious Life which God can give you. Christian — are you willing to enter in? Remember four things:

1. God has promised some better thing for us than a wilderness life of failure and discontent and doubt. He offers victory over known sin, and the enjoyment of wonderful communion with Him.

2. Our struggling and striving *cannot* give us that which God only can give.

3. We may and should bring our sins — the sins of Christian people — our doubts, our fears, our anxieties, our defeats, our weaknesses to Him, and trust the Lord Jesus to kill them; and then claim by faith Victory through Christ.

4. Then we can confidently say, "I now by faith *take* the

life of Victory, with all its rest and joy and fruitfulness.

"If ye be WILLING and obedient ye shall eat the good of the land."

Take another good look at that "land" — that LIFE — if you still hold back.

1. *It is a life of perfect rest.* "*Come* unto Me. . . . I will give you rest. Take My yoke upon you and LEARN OF ME — be My disciple — and ye shall find REST to your souls" (Matt. 11:28,29). All unrest dishonors Christ.

2. *It is a life of perfect peace.* "Peace I leave with you; My peace I give unto you" (John 14:27). To experience anything but peace — even under opposition, oppression, loss, bereavement, or perplexity — is to dishonor Christ and His Word.

Victory Follows Obedience

3. *It is a life of power.* "Ye shall receive power" (Acts 1:8). If we do not *possess* power we are dishonoring Christ. We are not waiting for God; GOD IS WAITING FOR US.

4. *It is a fruitful life.* "I can do all things through Christ Who strengtheneth me" (Phil. 4:13). A life of failure is dishonoring to Christ.

5. *It is a life lived by the Christ dwelling in us,* and therefore a life of perfect JOY.

In the wilderness God led His people — disobedient, rebellious, murmuring people — by a pillar of cloud and fire.

No sooner had they entered the land of promise than the Lord Jesus Christ Himself appeared to Joshua, not as one fighting for him, but as the Victorious Leader winning Victory so long as the people obeyed Him.

"Art thou for us or for our adversaries?" asks Joshua.

"Nay, but as captain of the host of the Lord am I NOW come" (Josh. 5:13,14). He was unable to come before. He could not come in this manner so long as the people wandered in the wilderness.

So with us. Christ will guide us — as with a cloud —

even when our lives are but a wilderness experience.

But when we are fully surrendered to Him He fills our hearts with His presence and takes complete control, and wins all our Victories for us — He, the captain of the host of the Lord.

Such a life is a Victorious Life — a life of constant miracle.